Napkin
Finance

Napkin
Finance

Build Your Wealth
in 30 Seconds or Less

TINA HAY

DEY ST.

An Imprint of WILLIAM MORROW

NAPKIN FINANCE. Copyright © 2019 by Tina Hay. All rights reserved. Printed in the United States of America. No part of this book may be used or reproduced in any manner whatsoever without written permission except in the case of brief quotations embodied in critical articles and reviews. For information, address HarperCollins Publishers, 195 Broadway, New York, NY 10007.

HarperCollins books may be purchased for educational, business, or sales promotional use. For information, please e-mail the Special Markets Department at SPsales@harpercollins.com.

FIRST EDITION

DESIGNED BY RENATA DE OLIVEIRA

Library of Congress Cataloging-in-Publication Data has been applied for.

ISBN 978-0-06-291503-0 (hardcover)
ISBN 978-0-06-298625-2 (international edition)

19 20 21 22 23   WOR   10 9 8 7 6 5 4 3 2 1

For Mehrzad and John Hay

Contents

Money 101

THE BASICS

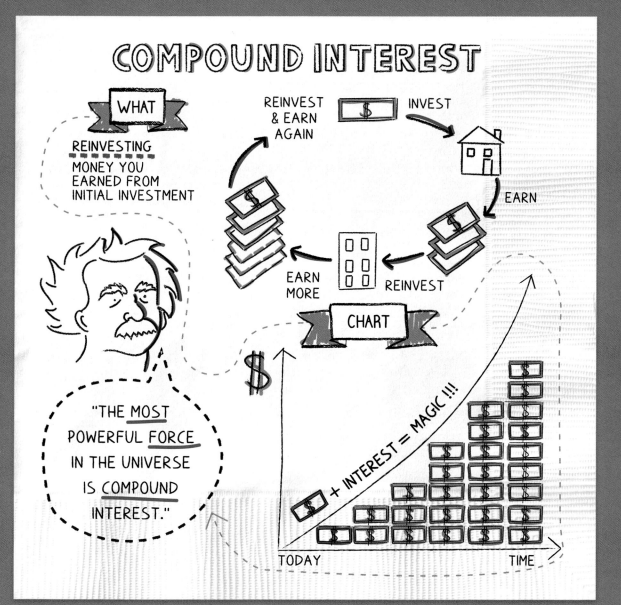

Compound Interest

You're probably familiar with the basic concept of earning interest: You put $1,000 in the bank, and the bank pays you a little bit in return, such as 2% per year. At the end of the year, you've earned $20.

If you leave that money in your account, in the second year you'll earn 2% on $1,020, not just on your original $1,000. And instead of earning $20, you'll earn $20 and 40 cents (you high roller, you). Compound interest refers to earning money on that growing balance (or put another way, earning interest on interest).

The magic of compounding is that your money grows exponentially. That extra 40 cents may not sound like much. But over time and with big enough numbers, compounding delivers mighty results.

$10,000 vs. $0.01

Would you rather receive $10,000 a day every day for a month or one penny that doubles each day for a month? (Hint: It's a trick question!)

Thanks to compounding, at the end of one month the doubling penny will have earned you $10,737,418 (and a massive need for some coin wrappers) compared with $310,000 if you had collected $10,000 per day.

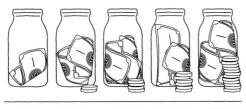

| DAY 1 | WEEK 1 | WEEK 2 | WEEK 3 | WEEK 4 |

$310,000

| DAY 1 | WEEK 1 | WEEK 2 | WEEK 3 | WEEK 4 |

$10,737,418

Boosting Your Money's Growth

Compounding always speeds along your money's growth (unless you withdraw your money instead of letting it continue to grow). But three main things can help turbo-charge your compounding:

› A higher interest rate
› Adding more money along the way
› Giving your money more time to grow

Fun Facts

› Compound interest is thought to have been invented in ancient Babylon around 2000 B.C., making it only slightly younger than the wheel.
› How many years will it take your money to double? Divide the number 72 by your interest rate to get a rough estimate. (It's called the "rule of 72." See chapter 12 for more information.)

Key Takeaways

› Compound interest is when you earn interest on interest (or pay interest on interest).
› Investors talk about the "magic of compounding" because of the incredible way it can grow your money.
› To increase your money's compounded growth, try to invest more money, let your money grow for a longer period, and find the best return rate you can.

I told my parents my allowance should pay compound interest and they told me to move out of the house cuz I'm in my thirties. —Napkin Finance ☺

Savings

Savings are funds that you put aside and don't spend.

Life can be full of surprises, both good and bad, but building savings is a great way to make sure you have cash available for emergencies, unexpected bills, medical expenses, and future goals. Most important, saving is key to building a lifetime of financial security.

> *"Do not save what is left after spending, but spend what is left after saving."*
>
> —WARREN BUFFETT, BILLIONAIRE INVESTOR

Benefits of Savings Accounts

Saving money is a great habit to get into. Keeping your hard-earned stash in a dedicated savings account also comes with certain benefits, including:

> › Stability—Savings accounts don't bounce around in value and won't lose money. They're for preserving what you have.
> › Growth—Your money grows in a savings account as you earn interest.
> › Safety—The U.S. government, through the Federal Deposit Insurance Corporation (FDIC), guarantees your balance at most banks for up to $250,000.

Saving Tips

> › Open a savings account.
>> › A dedicated savings account can help you keep your savings separate from your spending money, so you're not as tempted to dip into it. Choose an account with low or no fees and a high interest rate, and make sure you

can meet any minimum-balance requirements and live with any applicable restrictions on withdrawals.

› Pick a percentage.
   › Decide on a specific percentage of each paycheck that you will devote to savings based on your budget—even if it's as little as 1% to start. Experts suggest that ultimately you want to get to a 20% savings rate.
› Automate.
   › Set up a recurring automatic transfer from your checking account to your savings account. As soon as your paycheck is deposited, a portion of it should go straight into savings so that you don't have a chance to spend it.

Fun Facts

› Retail therapy is real. About half of Americans say emotions can drive them to overspend. Try not to take your stress out on your bank account.
› Paying with cash instead of a card can help you spend less. Apparently, counting out bills makes you feel the pain of spending more than swiping.
› Most Americans have less than $1,000 in savings. Ouch.

Key Takeaways

› Saving money for the future is a vital way of building up your financial security.
› Keeping your money in a savings account can let it earn interest, keep it safe, and help you avoid spending it.
› Setting up automatic transfers to your savings account and saving a dedicated percentage of your paycheck can help you get on track.

Save money on money by not spending it. —Napkin Finance ☺

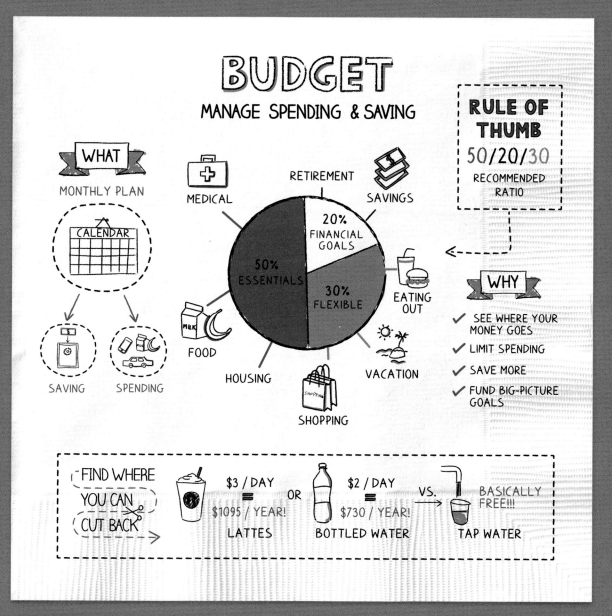

Budget

A budget is a plan you can use to better manage your spending and saving. When you follow a budget, you set limits on where your money goes. Following a budget can be a powerful way to improve your financial fortunes, because it helps ensure you're not spending more than you earn.

The benefits of budgeting include:

> *"Beware of little expenses. A small leak will sink a great ship."*
> —BENJAMIN FRANKLIN, FOUNDING FATHER

› Getting a clearer picture of where you actually spend your money (hello, takeout).
› Making sure you have enough money to meet your needs, while limiting how much you spend on your wants.
› Saving more money.
› Freeing up more money to pay down debt and fund other big-picture goals.

How to Make a Budget

Step 1: Figure out what you earn each month after tax.
Step 2: Track your expenses for a month or two to see how much you spend in a typical month and what you're spending it on. Tools such as worksheets and apps can help.
Step 3: Decide what categories you will use for your budget and come up with a monthly limit for each category, such as $200 per month for restaurants.

Step 4: Stick to your limits. Apps and software can also help you with this step—such as by alerting you when you've reached your limits for the month.

Step 5: Once you've gotten into the habit of watching your spending, try to find more places to cut back.

The 50–20–30 Budget

One big decision you need to make when budgeting is how much to dedicate to each spending category, as mentioned above.

One rule of thumb to consider is a 50–20–30 budget. With this approach, you divide your income into:

› 50% for essentials—including rent, utilities, groceries, and health care.
› 20% for financial goals—such as paying down debt, saving up a down payment, or funding your retirement.
› 30% for flexible spending—including entertainment, vacations, eating out, and nonessential purchases.

Fun Facts

› The word *budget* comes from the French word *bougette,* meaning "leather bag."
› In a year, the average American family spends $710 on their pets, $558 on alcohol, and only $110 on reading materials. #priorities

Key Takeaways

› A budget is a plan that lets you decide how much you spend and on what.

> Using a budget can be a powerful way to make sure you're living within your means.
> You can come up with a custom-made budget, or try a 50−20−30 budget.
> Apps can help you track your spending and stick to the limits you set.

If only everyone was as invested in budgeting as they are in finding a show to binge-watch on Netflix. —Napkin Finance ☺

Debt

Debt is money that you owe.

When you borrow money, you typically agree to pay it back over a certain period of time—called the loan's term. And you usually have to pay interest in addition to the original amount you borrowed.

You may use several types of debt at different points in your life. Some of the most common types include:

> Credit card—Any time you pay with a credit card, you are borrowing money. When you pay down your balance, you are paying off the debt.

> *"If you think nobody cares if you're alive, try missing a couple of car payments."*
>
> —EARL WILSON, WRITER

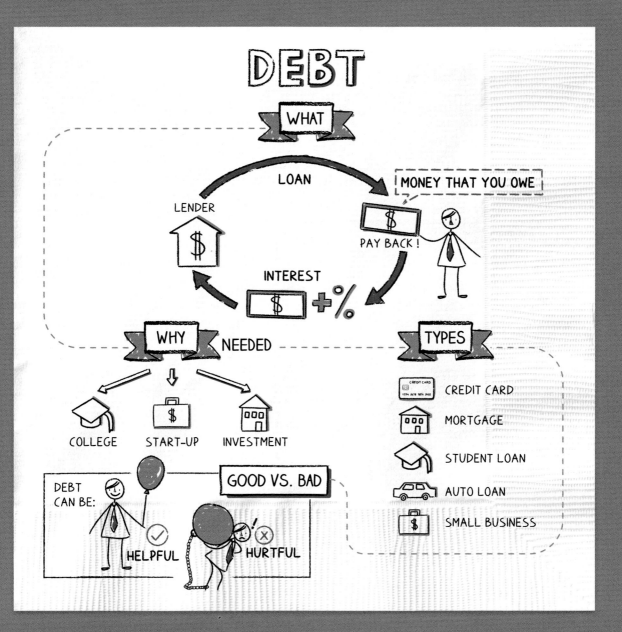

> Mortgage—A mortgage is a loan to buy real estate. A typical mortgage is paid back over a 15- or 30-year period.
> Student loan—You may take on student loans to pay for undergraduate or graduate school.
> Auto loan—An auto loan can help you buy a car.
> Small business—Companies borrow money too. Small-business loans can help new companies get off the ground.

Good Debt, Bad Debt

Whether a given debt is considered "good" or "bad" generally depends on the interest rate and whether you're taking on the debt in order to make a smart investment.

	Mortgage	Federal student loans	Credit card debt
Good or bad?	Good	Good	Bad
Interest rate	Low	Low	High
Smart investment?	Yes. There's a good chance your home will rise in value. Owning your own home can make you more financially secure.	Yes. A college education increases your earning power over the rest of your life.	No. That five-star prix fixe brunch you splurged on was amazing, but it won't pay any dividends.

Fun Facts

› American households carry more than $13 trillion in debt, including $9 trillion in mortgages, more than $1.5 trillion in student loans, and $1.2 trillion in auto loans.
› Twelve years is how long it would take for the average U.S. household that carries credit card debt to pay off its balances by making only the minimum payments.

Key Takeaways

› Debt is borrowed money that must be repaid, usually with interest.
› Chances are that at some point in your life you'll take on debt, such as student loans, credit card debt, or a mortgage.
› Whether debt is considered "good" or "bad" depends on whether it comes with a low or high interest rate and whether or not you're borrowing the money to make a good investment.

Not all debt is bad. Some is just misunderstood. —Napkin Finance ☺

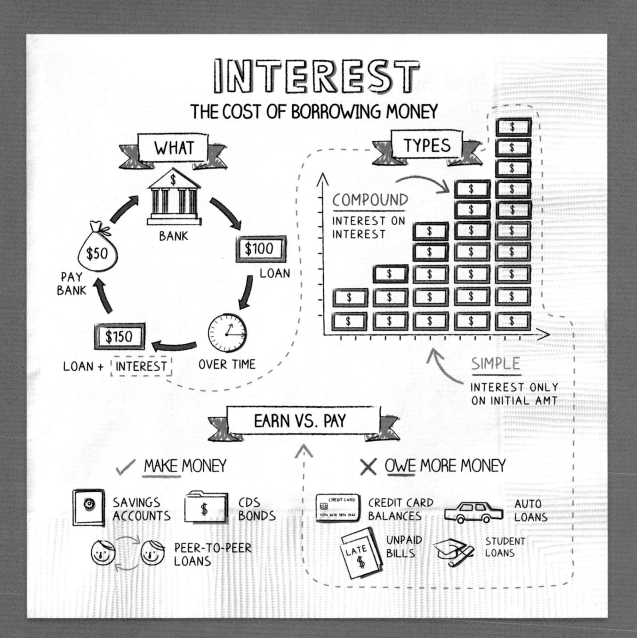

Interest

For a borrower, interest is the cost of taking on a loan. For a lender, interest is the profit earned on lending money.

Interest is expressed as a rate, such as 5%. How much interest the borrower pays is calculated by multiplying the rate by the amount borrowed and the length of time it takes to pay back the loan. For example, if you borrow $1,000 at a 5% interest rate for one year, you would pay back $1,050.

Interest Coming and Going

At different times in your life, you may be on the receiving or paying end of interest.

When you lend or invest money, a higher interest rate is better because it means you earn more. When you borrow money, a lower interest rate is better because it means you pay less.

You receive interest if:	You pay interest if:
You have money in an interest-bearing bank account.	You carry a balance on your credit card.
You own CDs, bonds, or other interest-bearing investments.	You borrow money to buy a house, go to college, or buy a car.
You make a peer-to-peer loan online, or a loan with interest to a friend.	You leave a bill unpaid and it starts to accrue interest.

Two Types of Interest

Simple interest is calculated only on the initial amount borrowed. *Compound interest* is calculated on the borrowed amount, plus on any accrued interest.

When you're comparing bank accounts or loan offers, you might see interest rates expressed as an "annual percentage rate" (APR) or "annual percentage yield" (APY). The former only expresses simple interest, while the latter reflects compounding.

The bottom line: Interest rates can be surprisingly complicated. Any time you're comparing rates—whether you're looking for a low rate to borrow at or a high rate to earn on your money—make sure you're comparing the same type of rate.

Fun Facts

› Although it's rare, interest rates can be negative—with the bank paying you to take out a loan (or charging you to keep your money safe).
› Islamic law prohibits paying or receiving interest. If you open a savings account with a Sharia-compliant bank, you may be offered a "target profit" instead of an interest rate.

Key Takeaways

› Interest is the cost of borrowing money.
› If you're borrowing money, interest works against you. If you're lending money, interest works for you.
› If you're ever comparing interest rates, make sure you're comparing the same type of rate.

You probably want a no-interest loan if you have no interest
in paying it back. —Napkin Finance ☺

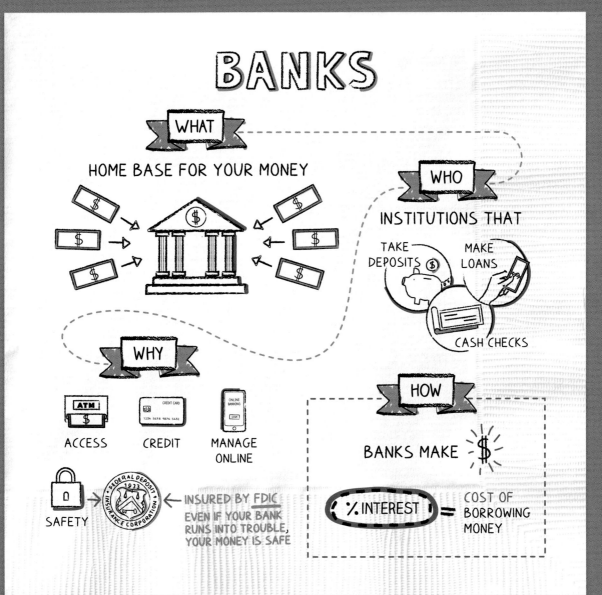

Banks

Banks are institutions that take deposits, cash checks, and make loans. They are essentially home bases for keeping your money safe and for making transactions.

Benefits of Banking

Using a bank account or other bank services can give you the advantages of:

> Safety—your money at the bank is typically insured for up to $250,000.
> Easy access—deposit and withdraw money conveniently.
> Online management—manage your accounts with your bank's website or app.
> Simple transfers—link your account to a payment app and it's easy to pay back your friend for those concert tickets.
> Access to loans—apply for a credit card or mortgage with your bank.

Safe and Secure

The money you deposit at a bank is safe. That's because the federal government, through the FDIC, insures bank accounts for up to a total of $250,000 per person, per institution. So even if your bank goes out of business (which is extremely unlikely) and your money disappears, you will be reimbursed up to that amount.

> *"A bank is a place that will lend you money if you can prove that you don't need it."*
> —BOB HOPE, ENTERTAINER

How Banks Make Money

Banks make loans to people and companies and charge interest on those loans (they also make money if you trigger fees on your account—learn your account's rules so you avoid that). Because they receive that interest income, banks are generally also able to pay a small amount of interest on money held in savings accounts.

Fun Facts

› At the Credito Emiliano bank in Italy, you can take out a loan using Parmesan cheese as collateral.
› Why would you rob a bank for just $1? To go to prison so you can get health care, according to the North Carolina man and Oregon man who (independently) tried to do just that in 2011 and 2013, respectively.

Key Takeaways

› Having a bank account can make it easier to manage your money.
› The money you hold at most banks is insured by the FDIC for up to $250,000, so your money is safe even if your bank goes under (RIP, Lehman Brothers).
› Banks make money by charging interest on loans.

Online banking is great if you want to transfer money from the comfort of your own bathtub. —Napkin Finance ☺

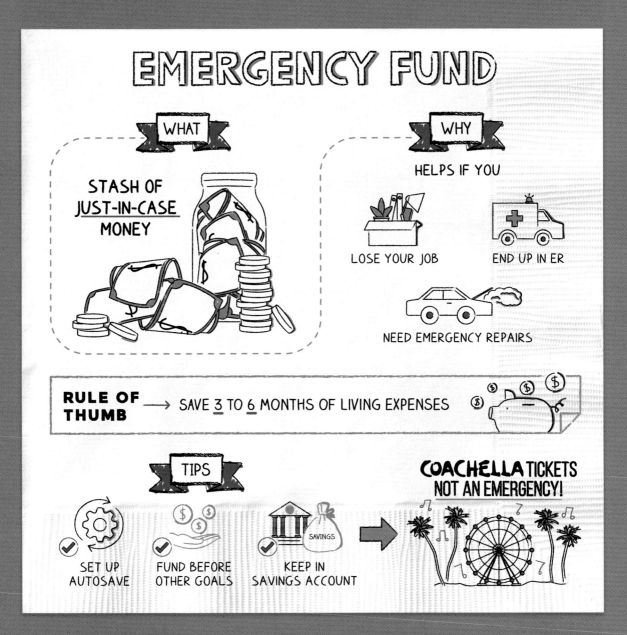

Emergency Fund

An emergency fund is your stash of *just-in-case* money.

Why Important

Your emergency fund is the money you would fall back on if:

> › You lost your job. › Your car broke down. › You ended up in the ER.

Having an emergency fund can help you roll with life's unpredictable punches, and makes it easier to recover from setbacks that could otherwise turn into financial disasters.

How to Build

Experts typically recommend that you keep three to six months of living expenses in your emergency fund (an amount that's probably less than three to six months of your income). However, you can potentially adjust that number up or down depending on certain factors.

Save less if:	Save more if:
You have stellar insurance coverage.	You have bare-bones insurance.
You could move back in with your parents in a heartbeat if you lost your job.	You'd sooner die than move in with family or onto a friend's couch.
You fly solo in life.	You have kids or other dependents.
You have plenty of other assets.	Your finances are already precarious.

Tips

Best practices for your emergency fund include:

> › Making it a priority. Many experts recommend that you build up your emergency fund before you tackle other goals, such as saving for retirement.
> › Keeping it in a savings account—where it will be safe and easy to access, but can still earn some interest.
> › Setting up automatic transfers from your checking account to your emergency fund until it's fully funded.

When to Use

Last-minute Coachella tickets may feel like an emergency—but sorry, they don't count. Don't crack open your emergency piggy bank unless the bill you're facing is truly an emergency.

You should also try not to use your emergency fund for predictable expenses. If you know your car's going to call it quits soon, build up a separate new car fund so you don't have to raid your emergency savings when the time comes.

Fun Facts

> › About two in five adults don't have the cash to cover a $400 unexpected bill.
> › The most common reason people give for tapping their emergency fund is to pay for home repairs, followed by car repairs.

Key Takeaways

> › An emergency fund is just what it sounds like: a savings fund for emergency expenses.
> › Try to save three to six months of living expenses in your emergency fund.

> Your emergency fund should be held somewhere easy to access, such as a savings account (see Savings section earlier in this chapter).

It's important to have an emergency fund in case of unexpected unemployment. It's important to have a barf bag and pickles in case of an unexpected pregnancy. —Napkin Finance ☺

Insurance

Insurance is financial protection. Along with your emergency fund, insurance makes up your safety net so that any number of potential disasters—such as an accident, illness, fire in your home, or death in your family—don't wreck your financial security.

When you buy an insurance policy, you usually agree to periodically pay the insurer a certain amount of money—called a premium. In exchange, the insurer promises to pay you back or help cover your costs if you ever need to make a claim or file for reimbursement for covered losses.

At Every Life Stage

Your insurance needs typically change with major life events and milestones. On page 25, you'll see some of the types of insurance you may need at different points in your life.

Tips

> Lower risk equals lower premiums. If you don't smoke, your chances of dying from smoking-related diseases are lower, so you can typically obtain a cheaper life insurance policy.

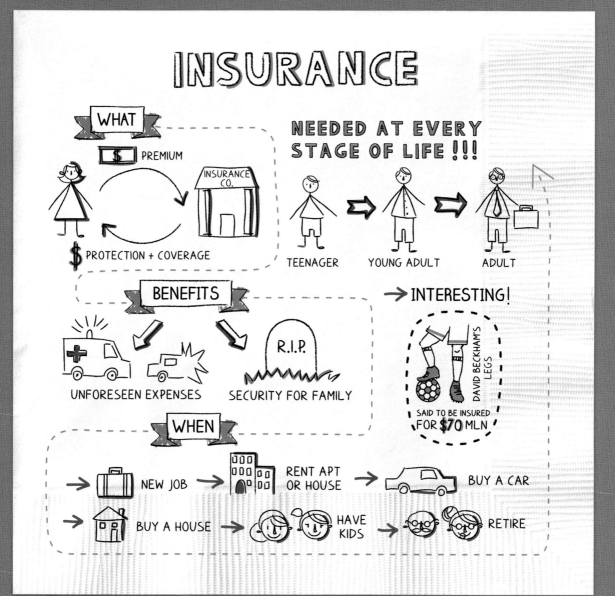

> Learn about your deductibles—amounts that you often must pay out of pocket before your insurance pays anything.
> If you make a lot of claims, your premiums may go up. This is why people in fender benders often don't tell their car insurance company.
> Insurance is complicated and can vary a lot from policy to policy. Read your contracts closely so that you understand your coverage.

Milestone	Insurance need
Landing your first job	Welcome to the world of navigating your own health insurance.
Renting your first apartment	Hello, renters insurance.
Buying a car	In most states, you cannot legally drive without auto insurance.
Buying a home	Goodbye, renters insurance. Hello, title, mortgage, and property insurance. (Flood coverage is extra.)
Having kids	Congratulations! Each little bundle of joy needs to be added to your health insurance. You'd also better get yourself some life insurance.

Fun Facts

> At the height of his soccer career, David Beckham's legs were said to be insured for $70 million.
> Actress Shirley MacLaine reportedly owns a $25 million insurance policy protecting her fortune against alien abduction.

Key Takeaways

› When you buy an insurance policy, you agree to pay the insurer a small amount of money regularly. In exchange, the insurance company agrees to pay you a large amount of money if something horrible happens.

› You may need new insurance any time you hit a major life milestone, such as having kids or buying a house.

› Insurance companies charge more for riskier policies.

An apple a day keeps the doctor away. And so does not having health insurance. —Napkin Finance ☺

Chapter Quiz

1. Your money in the bank is safe because:

a. It's kept inside a safe, literally.
b. The bank told you it was, and why would they lie???
c. The CEO of the bank personally guarantees every dollar you deposit.
d. It's insured by the federal government for up to $250,000.

2. Banks make money by:

a. Charging interest on loans.
b. Repossessing houses.
c. Laundering money on the side.
d. Sending their chairman to Vegas with a bag of cash once a month.

3. **The benefits of budgeting include all of the following, except:**

    a. Helping you learn to live within your means.

    b. Increasing your Social Security income in retirement.

    c. Letting you see where your money actually goes.

    d. Helping you set aside more money to put toward your goals.

4. **One favored rule-of-thumb budget is the:**

    a. 10–90 budget: 10% rent, 90% Girl Scout cookies.

    b. 40–20–40 budget: 40% housing, 20% food, 40% everything else.

    c. 50–20–30 budget: 50% essentials, 20% goals, 30% flexible.

    d. 10–10–80 budget: 10% bars, 10% Ubers, 80% good times.

5. **Compound interest is:**

    a. Earning interest on the interest you already earned.

    b. An amount a stock pays every month.

    c. A thing to mention at parties to sound smart.

    d. When you're more invested in the characters by season two of a show than you were in season one.

6. **True or false: Receiving $10,000 every day for a month is better than receiving a penny that doubles every day for a month.**

    ○ True   ○ False

7. **The key to letting compounding work its magic is to:**

    a. Send it to Hogwarts.

    b. Check the "Yes, I want to earn compound interest" box when you open your account.

    c. Not withdraw the money you earn, and instead let it continue to grow.

    d. Not wash your hair for at least 30 minutes after you put the compound in.

8. **Common types of debt include all of the following except:**

    a. Student loans.
    b. Small-business loans.
    c. Garden-variety loans.
    d. Mortgage loans.

9. **Debt might be "good debt" if it:**

    a. Comes with a low interest rate and pays for a smart investment.
    b. Was a lot of fun to spend the money.
    c. Is less than $500.
    d. Taught you a nice lesson about what truly matters. Awww.

10. **True or false: You should keep three to six months of living expenses in your emergency fund.**

    ◯ True   ◯ False

11. **It's okay to dip into your emergency fund if you:**

    a. Need to make it to your best friend's bachelorette party.
    b. Get a new job and need to invest in a new wardrobe.
    c. Want to go to Whole Foods for lunch.
    d. Lose your job and need to pay for health insurance out of pocket.

12. **You may be able to lower your insurance premiums by:**

    a. Paying more in "points" when you take out your policy.
    b. Staying healthy and avoiding making insurance claims unless you really have to.
    c. Moving to Canada.
    d. Selling your life insurance policy to the highest bidder.

13. When you borrow money, you should seek out:

- a. Some new ripped friends to protect you when you never pay the money back.
- b. A high rate of interest, because no one will realistically expect you to pay back the loan.
- c. A low rate of interest, because a low-interest loan pays you a bigger return.
- d. A low rate of interest, so that you pay less.

14. Simple interest is:

- a. Interest that never graduated eighth grade.
- b. Interest earned only on the initial amount borrowed—in contrast to compound interest.
- c. A cool band that new intern at work seems to enjoy.
- d. Interest that just isn't looking for a commitment right now.

15. True or false: You don't need to worry about saving money until you're at least forty.

○ True ○ False

16. You can help yourself save more by doing all of the following, except:

- a. Saving in a savings account.
- b. Setting up automatic transfers to your savings account.
- c. Aiming to save a specific percent of your paycheck each month.
- d. Having children.

Answers

1. d	**5.** a	**9.** a	**13.** d
2. a	**6.** f	**10.** t	**14.** b
3. b	**7.** c	**11.** d	**15.** f
4. c	**8.** c	**12.** b	**16.** d

2

Credit Where It's Due

BUILDING CREDIT

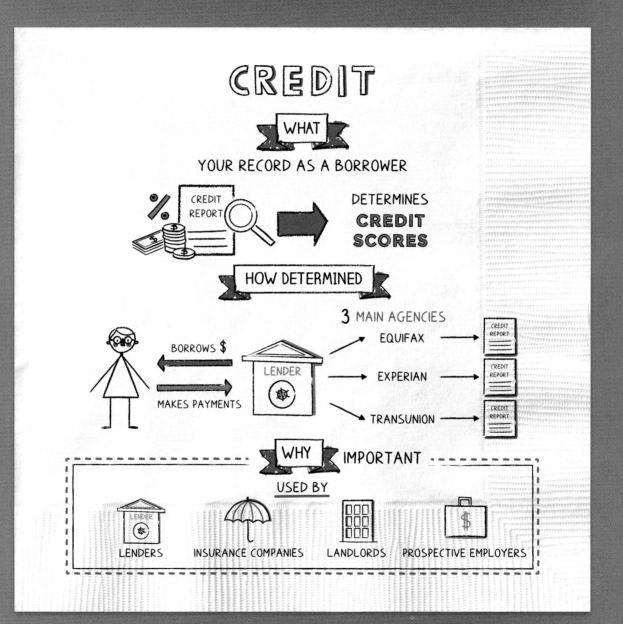

Credit

Credit is, simply put, your financial reputation. Your credit history describes your record as a borrower, including whether you've generally paid bills on time or not.

Why Important

Your credit history can be used for many reasons, including by:

> › Lenders, in deciding whether to loan you money.
> › Lenders, in deciding what interest rate to charge you.
> › Insurance companies, in setting what rate to charge you.
> › Landlords, in deciding whether to rent to you.
> › Prospective employers, in deciding whether to hire you.

How to Build Credit

You generally build credit any time you borrow money. Repaying money as promised helps you build good credit. Missing payments builds a poor credit history. Actions that affect your credit can include:

> › Spending on your credit card and paying your monthly bill.
> › Making or missing your student loan payments.
> › Making or missing payments on any other type of debt, including a car loan or mortgage.
> › Unresolved overdrafts on your bank account.
> › Unpaid utility bills or doctor bills. (Yep, really.)
> › Any time a bill goes to collections.

Who Keeps Track of Your Credit?

Private companies called "credit bureaus" keep track of your credit history. If you miss a credit card payment, your card issuer will probably report the missed payment to the bureaus. (Sometimes, it's possible to persuade a lender not to report a missed payment.) The three main credit bureaus are:

> › Equifax   › Experian   › TransUnion

The credit bureaus keep track of everything that's reported to them for seven years (after seven years, negative marks generally get erased). That information is called your "credit report," and it's used to calculate your credit scores.

Fun Facts

› Both Equifax and Experian started as groups of business owners who decided to share notes on which of their customers weren't paying their debts.
› Equifax allegedly used to collect information on consumers' marriages, political activities, and even "bedroom activities" (wink wink).

Key Takeaways

› Your credit and credit history describe your record as a borrower.
› Credit is important because it can affect your ability to obtain loans or even get hired for a job.
› Lenders report information about how much you borrow and whether you repay debts on time to credit bureaus, which compile this information into your credit reports.

How you treat waiters should affect your credit scores. —Napkin Finance ☺

Credit Cards

A credit card lets you buy now and pay later, all without the hassle of counting out bills or change. When you spend on a credit card you are borrowing from the issuer (such as the bank that issued your card). At any given point in time, your card balance is the total amount you currently owe.

Credit cards generally come with a set limit—the maximum balance you can carry—such as $5,000. If you try to spend beyond your limit, your card will probably be declined.

What If Overdue?

As with any other type of debt, you need to make your credit card payments on time. Interest will start to accrue on any balance that you carry from one month to the next. And if you don't at least make your minimum payment, your account will probably also start to accrue fees. Missing credit card payments is a surefire way of tanking your credit score, fast.

Benefits of Credit Cards

If you're careful with your plastic, credit cards can offer the following advantages:

> › Easy to use online
> › Offer solid protections if your card is lost or stolen
> › May let you earn rewards, such as points, miles, or cash back
> › Can help you build your credit history

Credit vs. Debit Cards

Although you can generally use credit and debit cards the same way—whether swiping at the store or placing an order online—they have some important differences.

	Credit cards	Debit cards
What?	Spend borrowed money that you have to repay later.	Spend directly from your bank account.
Owe interest?	Pay interest on any balance you carry month to month.	Pay no interest.
Earn rewards?	Yes, with a rewards card.	Typically, no.
Impact on your credit history?	Build good credit if you pay on time or bad credit if you don't.	No impact.
Difficult to obtain?	Have to pass a credit check to get one.	Generally, qualify automatically when you open a bank account.

Fun Facts

› There are almost 400 million open credit cards in the U.S.—a little more than one for every person.
› Until 1974, women needed their husbands to cosign to get a credit card. The Equal Credit Opportunity Act then banned discrimination in issuing credit. (Women are still charged higher interest rates, on average.)

Key Takeaways

› When you spend with a credit card, you are taking out a loan.

> As with any other type of borrowed money, you need to pay your credit card bills on time or else interest and fees may accrue.
> Credit cards and debit cards may look almost identical, but have important differences in terms of interest charges, effects on your credit history, and the potential to earn rewards.

Identity theft would be less scary if instead of stealing money they just take your credit card and raise your kids. —Napkin Finance ☺

Improving Credit

Your credit report and credit scores describe whether you have a good track record of repaying borrowed money. Lenders and others may use your credit history to get a sense of whether you're likely to fulfill your financial obligations. With a good credit history, it can be easier to open a credit card, get an apartment or a mortgage, or even get hired for a job.

How to Improve

Whether you already have a flawless credit history or you're financially challenged, try taking these steps to boost your score:

> Pay all bills on time.
> Pay your credit card off in full each month.
> Check your credit report periodically for errors, such as debt marked as unpaid that you actually did pay off. (You're entitled to a free report from each of the three main credit bureaus once per year.)

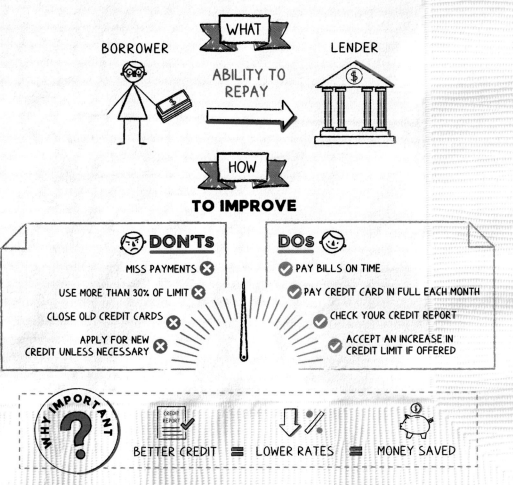

> Accept any increases in your credit limit that your issuer offers you.

To protect your history and score, you should also try not to:

> Miss payments (not just on your credit cards, but on anything).
> Use more than 30% of your credit limit on any given card.
> Close old credit cards.
> Apply for new credit unless you're sure it's the right move.

Why Important

A good credit score can save you real money by qualifying you for better interest rates on loans.

Consider two mortgage borrowers, both looking to borrow $200,000 over 30 years. The borrower with the better credit score could save as much as $100,000 in interest payments over the life of the loan.

	Term	Amount	Interest rate	Monthly payment	Total interest
Good credit	30 years	$200,000	5%	$1,074	$186,512
Poor credit	30 years	$200,000	7.5%	$1,398	$303,434

Fun Facts

> The word *credit* comes from the Latin word *credere,* which means "to trust."
> Improving your credit could mean improving your romantic prospects if you use CreditScoreDating.com, a dating site for people who care a lot about prospective suitors' financial histories.

Key Takeaways

> To improve your credit, make sure you pay all your bills on time and pay off your credit card balance in full each month.
> It can also help to avoid applying for new credit, closing old cards, and using more than 30% of your credit limit on a given card.
> Having good credit can make it easier to borrow money or rent an apartment, but it can also save you real money when it comes to taking on a mortgage or other large loan.

Rome and Beyoncé weren't built in a day, and neither is good credit.
—Napkin Finance ☺

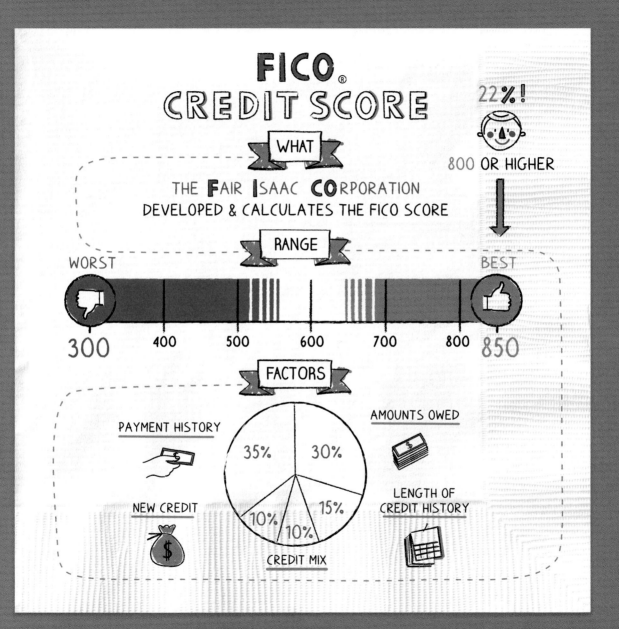

FICO® Credit Score

Although you might hear the phrase "your credit score" tossed around, you actually have multiple credit scores—potentially hundreds. Of these, a FICO score is probably the most common and the most well-known. It's named for the company that calculates the score: the Fair Isaac Corporation.

What's a Good FICO Score?

FICO scores can range from 300 to 850—the higher, the better.

Score range	How good?	What percentage of people score in this range?
800–850	Amazing!	22%
700–799	Solid	36%
600–699	Not great	23%
300–599	Yikes	19%

What Goes into Your Score

There are five main factors that go into your FICO score, and some are more important than others:

Factor	Weighting in your score	What is it?
Payment history	35% Most important	Have you made payments on time in the past, or have you missed payments?
Amounts owed	30% Very important	Do you max out your cards, or only use a small portion of your total credit limit?
Length of credit history	15% Less important	Do you have a long or short credit history? (Longer is better.)
New credit	10% Least important	Have you applied for 20 new credit cards in the last month, or do you use new credit sparingly?
Credit mix	10% Least important	Have you only ever managed a credit card, or do you also have a track record with student loans, a mortgage, or other types of loans?

Fun Facts

› It's not called the "Fair Isaac" company to advertise that the scores are fair. It's because the company founders' names were William Fair and Earl Isaac. (And "William-Earl Score" is much less catchy.)

› The "UltraFICO" score is a new type of credit score that considers how much cash you have in the bank. It may be helpful for people with spotty or no credit histories.

Key Takeaways

› A FICO score is probably the most common and well-known type of credit score.

› FICO scores can range from 300 to 850. The higher your score, the better.

› The most important factor to your FICO score is whether you have a good record of repaying borrowed money in the past. How much you borrow, the length of your credit history, and other factors also matter.

Nothing is more unattractive than bad breath or a subprime FICO score.
—Napkin Finance ☺

Chapter Quiz

1. Credit is:

a. The name of the person who invented the credit card.
b. Your criminal record.
c. Your reputation as a borrower.
d. A sequel to the *Rocky* movies.

2. The three credit bureaus include all the following, except:

a. Transamerica.
b. TransUnion.
c. Equifax.
d. Experian.

3. **True or false: An unpaid medical bill can wind up as a ding on your credit report.**

   ○ True   ○ False

4. **Things you can do to improve your credit include all of the following, except:**

   a. Paying your bills.
   b. Opening a new credit card every time a store clerk offers you one.
   c. Paying your credit card balance in full each month.
   d. Checking your credit report for errors periodically.

5. **Things you shouldn't do because they'll hurt your credit score include all of the following, except:**

   a. Missing payments.
   b. Maxing out your cards.
   c. Freezing your credit card in a block of ice so you can't use it.
   d. Opening a new credit card every time a store clerk offers you one.

6. **Your credit history and credit score may be used when:**

   a. You're applying for a job.
   b. You're buying a new car with cash.
   c. Your teacher offers extra credit on a test.
   d. You're writing your marriage vows.

7. **True or false: Closing old cards you don't use anymore can help your credit score.**

   ○ True   ○ False

8. **When you pay with a credit card you are:**
   a. Having a great time waiting for the chip reader to work.
   b. Showing off how wealthy, fabulous, and carefree you are.
   c. Spending Monopoly money. It's not even real!
   d. Borrowing money from the credit card issuer that you'll have to repay.

9. **Missing a credit card payment is:**
   a. Playing hard to get.
   b. Not a big deal if you don't do it more than once a year.
   c. Literal death.
   d. A big deal, and something you should avoid, but something your life can recover from.

10. **True or false: Using credit cards responsibly can help you build a good credit history.**
    ○ True   ○ False

11. **True or false: Spending with a debit card typically lets you earn more rewards points.**
    ○ True   ○ False

12. **Your FICO score is:**
    a. The single determinant of whether you will be a successful and happy person in life.
    b. The most well-known type of credit score.
    c. An index of your salary.
    d. The highest score you can earn on Fortnite.

13. **A great FICO score range is:**

    a. 0–100.

    b. 900–1,000.

    c. 800–850.

    d. 867–5309 ("Jenny, I Got Your FICO Score").

14. **True or false: A short credit history is better because it shows you use credit sparingly.**

    ○ True   ○ False

15. **FICO stands for:**

    a. Falling Into Cave Openings.

    b. The Finally, I Can Open a credit card Act.

    c. The Federal Insurance Contributions Organization.

    d. The Fair Isaac Corporation.

Answers

1. c	**4.** b	**7.** f	**10.** t	**13.** c
2. a	**5.** c	**8.** d	**11.** f	**14.** f
3. t	**6.** a	**9.** d	**12.** b	**15.** d

3

Buy Low, Sell High

INVESTING

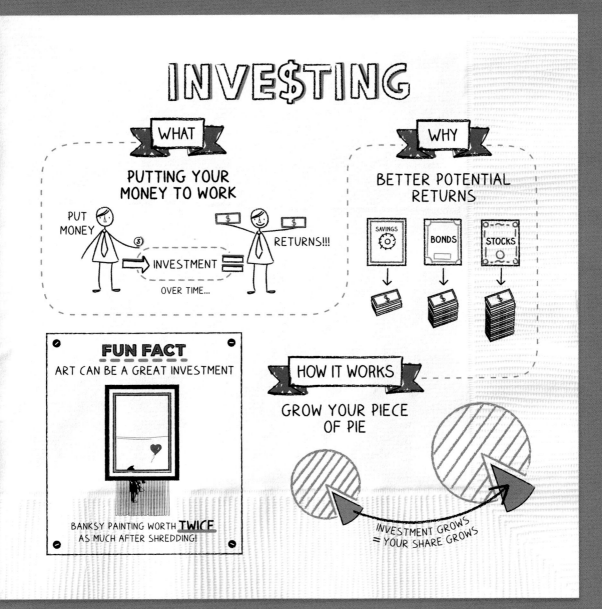

Investing

Investing is putting your money to work in the hopes of earning a return.

You probably already invest in all kinds of things. When you invest in your education, the return you're hoping to earn may be higher future pay or a promising job. When you invest in some designer shoes, you might be hoping to earn a return in compliments or social status.

When it comes to your finances, though, investing refers to putting your money to work in stocks, bonds, or some other kind of venture, in the hopes of earning a profit.

"How many millionaires do you know who have become wealthy by investing in savings accounts?"

—ROBERT G. ALLEN, INVESTOR AND AUTHOR

Why Invest?

Investing can be a powerful way to grow your wealth, because investments such as stocks and mutual funds have historically provided great returns over long periods. Consider how your money would grow if you kept it in a savings account earning 0.1% interest versus if you invested it in U.S. stocks, which have a long-term average annual return rate of 10%.

	Initial investment	Return rate	Invested for	Ending amount
Savings	$10,000	0.1%/year	20 years	$10,202
Stocks	$10,000	10%/year	20 years	$67,275

Of course, in the real world investments can go down as well as up, and they don't usually deliver smooth returns every year. But in the long run, investing usually grows your money faster than the alternatives.

How Investing Works

The stock market generally goes up over the long run because the economy is usually growing—thanks to population growth and to advancements in technology. More people in the world means more people buying things. And technological advancements can improve workers' productivity and foster new discoveries. Both of those factors help companies sell more stuff and earn bigger profits over time. Investing lets you get a piece of the pie.

Here's the basic process:

Step 1: You invest by buying an ownership stake in a company (such as by buying a stock) or loaning the company money (such as by buying a bond).

Step 2: The company sells its products and grows.

Step 3: Your ownership stake is now worth more, so you can sell it for a profit. Or, the company repays the money it borrowed from you, with interest.

Investing is more than just the stock market. You can invest in real estate, currency, vintage cars, fine art, and more.

Fun Facts

› Art can make a great investment. Banksy's *Girl with Balloon* painting reportedly doubled in value after it self-destructed at a Sotheby's auction in 2018.

› You don't have to start rich to get rich. Warren Buffett's fortune started with his earnings from his newspaper route. He made his first stock investment at age eleven (it was Cities Service, an oil company that eventually became Citgo).

Key Takeaways

› Investing is putting your money to work in the hopes of earning a profit or return.

› Putting your money into stocks, bonds, and other investments can provide powerful growth over time.

› Investing works because the economy grows over time, which means companies sell more stuff and earn bigger profits.

Call your broker if you want advice about your investments, and call your mom if you want unsolicited advice about your life. —Napkin Finance ☺

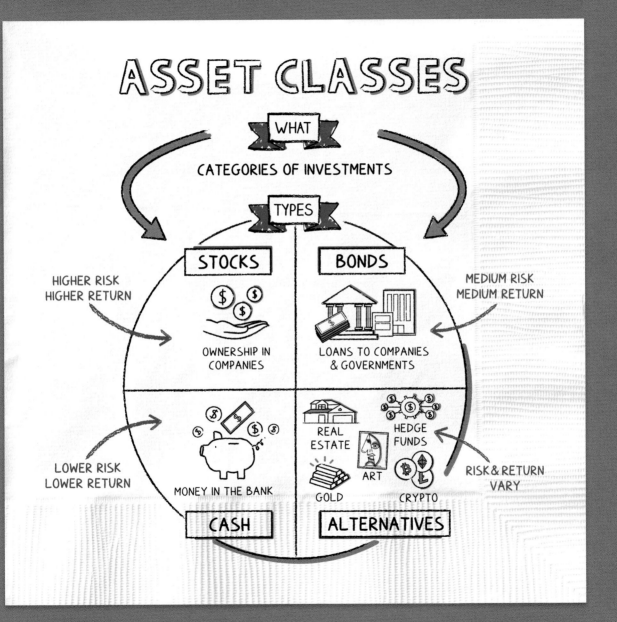

Asset Classes

Asset classes are major categories of investments. They're the building blocks of investing, which you can use to create a portfolio, or well-rounded group of investments.

Main Asset Classes

Stocks

› When you buy a stock, you become a part-owner in a company.
› You earn a return if the stock goes up in value—which typically happens if the company's profits increase.
› Some stocks also pay dividends—a small amount of cash or shares that are distributed to shareholders periodically.
› Many, but not all, trade on stock exchanges such as the New York Stock Exchange (NYSE). Some others trade informally through networks of dealers.

Bonds

› When you buy a bond, you become a lender to the entity that issued the bond—typically a corporation or government entity.
› With most bonds, you earn a return when the bond pays interest.
› Usually, you receive your initial investment back when the bond matures.
› Bonds don't typically trade on exchanges, but you can still buy or sell them from brokerages.

Cash

› Cash includes the stuff in your wallet as well as your money at the bank.
› If you hold your cash in an account that pays interest, you'll earn a small return on your cash.
› Unlike stocks and bonds, your cash at the bank is typically insured for up to $250,000, so it's safe.

Alternatives

› Alternative investments can include real estate, hedge funds, private equity, cryptocurrencies, commodities such as gold, or anything else that doesn't fit neatly into another bucket.
› With real estate, you may earn a return when your tenants pay rent.
› Other types of alternatives, such as cryptocurrencies and gold, don't pay out any returns. Instead, investors are betting that the cryptocurrency, gold, or other asset they own will rise in price.

Fun Facts

› If you can dream it, there's a way to invest in it: There have been investment funds that bet on the weather, that bet on prices of ancient Chinese pottery, and that bet on people dying.
› Although real estate is sometimes touted as a surefire investment, stocks have produced better long-term returns.

Key Takeaways

› Asset classes, such as stocks and bonds, are the building blocks of investing.

> A stock is an ownership stake in a company, and usually gains in value if the company's profits rise.
> A bond is a loan to a company or other entity, and pays a return as long as the borrower pays its debts.
> Many other investments fall under the catchall category of alternative investments.

Typical asset classes include stocks, bonds, real estate, cash, and no asses whatsoever. —Napkin Finance ☺

Diversification

Diversification is the practice of dividing your money among lots of different types of investments. It's the investing version of spreading your bets.

Benefits of Diversification

Investing experts disagree about a lot of things, but they tend to agree that diversifying is a great strategy. Here are some of the advantages:

> Reduced risk. The more you spread your money around, the less you stand to lose if any one or two of your investments tank.

"Don't look for the needle in the haystack. Just buy the haystack."

—JOHN BOGLE,
INVENTOR OF INDEX INVESTING

DIVERSIFICATION

WHAT

A WAY TO MINIMIZE RISK

STOCKS

BONDS

$

CASH

ALTERNATIVES

BY SPREADING OUT INVESTMENTS

WAYS

ASSET CLASSES   GEOGRAPHY   INDUSTRY   COMPANY SIZE

AKA

DON'T PUT ALL YOUR EGGS IN ONE BASKET!!

> › Better chances at finding winners. Every investor wants to get in on the next Google or Amazon. The more investments you own, the better your chances of doing so.
> › Smoother returns. Any one investment might rise or fall in price from year to year. But holding a broad range usually reduces the bumps.

Ways to Diversify

You can diversify according to:

Asset classes	Consider holding a mix of stocks, bonds, cash, and alternative investments.
Geography	The U.S. can be a great place to invest, but other countries' investments may offer better returns when the U.S. hits a recession.
Industry	In some years, tech companies may be the best-performing investments, while in other years oil companies (or another industry) may be. It can make sense to hold a bit of everything.
Bond issuer type	For your bond investments, consider holding a mix of corporate, federal government, and state and local government bonds.
Company size	Small companies tend to do better during strong economies, while larger companies tend to do better during recessions. Consider investing in both.

Fun Facts

> › The word *diversification* comes from the Latin words *diversus,* meaning "turned in different ways," and *faciō,* meaning "to make" or "to do."

› Some investors diversify with precious metals. Gold often performs well during stock market crashes, when investors are looking for safe havens.

Key Takeaways

› Diversifying is the act of spreading your money around with many kinds of investments.
› The benefits of diversification can include reduced risk, better chances at holding winners, and smoother performance.
› You can diversify by investing in different asset classes, countries, and industries, among other ways.

Diversification is a great investment strategy as well as a delicious cheese platter strategy. —Napkin Finance 😊

Risk vs. Reward

All investments come with risk. With financial investments, risk is usually tied to reward. That means investments with the potential to return the most also usually have the potential to lose the most. And safe investments typically don't return much.

What Is Risk?

Investors often think of risk as how much an investment bounces around in price, which is called volatility.

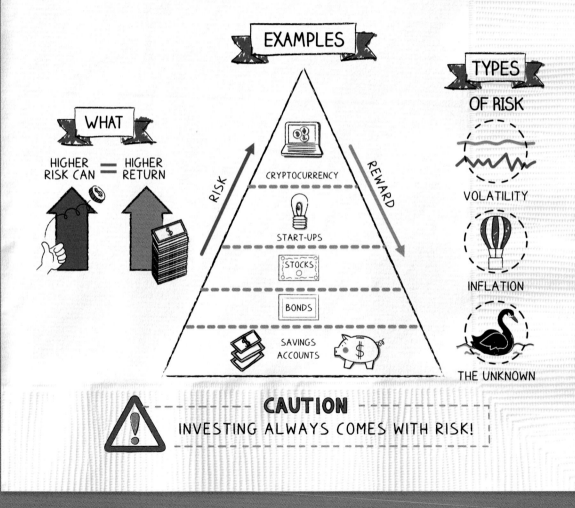

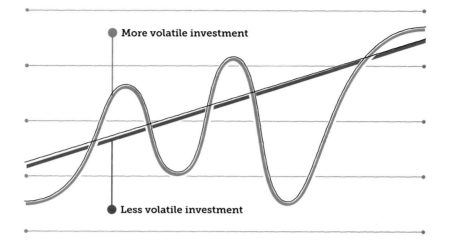

More volatile investment

Less volatile investment

Some experts argue that volatility doesn't capture all types of risk. For one thing, investors' accounts with Bernie Madoff (who ran one of the largest investment frauds in history) showed pretty smooth returns. And technically, an investment that consistently loses money could be "low risk" under this definition.

But volatility is still the best shortcut for understanding which investments are high risk and which are low risk.

Investments According to Risk/Return

Since risk and reward go hand in hand, you can rank investment types according to their risk and potential return:

Investment type	Risk level	Why?
Cryptocurrency	XXXXX	Some cryptocurrencies end up being worthless. Others could turn you into a millionaire overnight.
Start-ups	XXXX	Some start-ups will be wildly successful, some will flame out, and others will fall somewhere in the middle.
Stocks	XXX	Stocks can ping-pong in price and occasionally take a nosedive, but in the long term they usually deliver solid returns—at about 10% per year on average.
Bonds	XX	Bonds can rise or fall in price, but usually much less than stocks. Long-term they've earned about 5% per year on average.
Savings accounts	X	Savings accounts are federally insured for up to $250,000, so you have a 0% chance of losing money if you stay within that limit. But you might only earn 0.1% per year.

Choosing the right balance of risk and return is arguably the most important part of investing. Your risk/reward balance is described by your asset allocation—a topic we turn to next.

Fun Facts

› Despite the risk/reward relationship, women tend to invest more conservatively than men but still earn better returns (on average)— possibly because they trade less.

> Remember the point that if you can dream it, you can invest in it? Some strategies can let you invest in volatility itself—meaning you make money when the market acts bananas and lose money when it's calm.

Key Takeaways

> Investing always comes with risk.
> Usually, investments that have the potential to return more are riskier.
> Many investors think of risk as how much an investment swings in price, but there can be other types of risk too.

It's important to weigh the risks versus rewards when it comes to investing and getting lunch from a food truck. —Napkin Finance ☉

Asset Allocation

"Asset allocation" is a way of describing what you own in percentage terms. If you've got $1,000 to your name and it's all sitting in your checking account, you have a 100% allocation to cash. If you're worth $10,000 and half of that is in your shoe collection, you have a 50% allocation to shoes (and a 100% commitment to looking fabulous).

When people talk about asset allocation, they're usually referring to investment accounts. Choosing the right asset allocation is mainly about choosing the right amount of risk to take on.

Benefits

The advantages of choosing a well-suited asset allocation can include:

ASSET ALLOCATION

WHAT

DIVIDING YOUR $$
INTO DIFFERENT ASSET CLASSES

STOCKS

BONDS

PORTFOLIO

CASH

OTHER

RULE OF THUMB

HOW

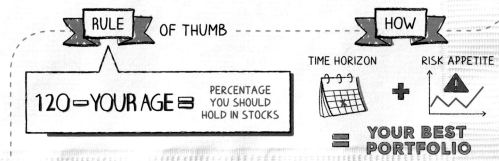

$$120 - \text{YOUR AGE} = \text{PERCENTAGE YOU SHOULD HOLD IN STOCKS}$$

TIME HORIZON + RISK APPETITE

= **YOUR BEST PORTFOLIO**

✔ **BENEFITS** — ✔ BOOST RETURNS — ✔ REDUCE RISK — ✔ GAIN CONFIDENCE — ✔ STICK WITH PLAN

- › Boosting your returns.
- › Reducing your portfolio's risk.
- › Helping you feel more confident in your strategy.
- › Making it easier to stick with an investing plan (which also helps your returns).

Figuring Out Your Asset Allocation

Two main factors should determine your asset allocation: your time horizon and your personal risk appetite.

- › Time horizon—The longer you have before you'll need to sell your investments, the more risk you can take on. That's because with a longer time horizon you can wait for your investments to bounce back if the market falls off a cliff.
- › Risk appetite—If you think that seeing your investments tank would give you a panic attack, you probably don't want to hold very risky investments. If you can live with some price swings, you can take on more risk.

Putting It All Together

Once you've figured out how much risk to take on, you can choose a high-level asset allocation. (See the examples on the following page.)

Fun Facts

- › Warren Buffett likes to keep asset allocation simple. He has said that a portfolio with 90% of assets invested in an S&P 500 index fund and

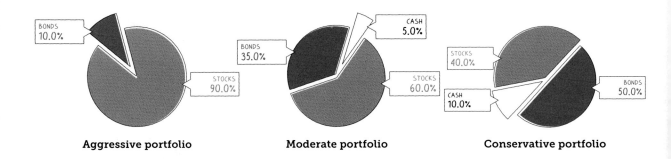

Aggressive portfolio   **Moderate portfolio**   **Conservative portfolio**

10% invested in Treasury bonds will usually beat the results of high-priced money managers.

> A quick rule of thumb when choosing your asset allocation is to subtract your age from 120. That number is how much you should hold in stocks. Put the rest in bonds.

Key Takeaways

> Asset allocation is a high-level description of your investments in percentage terms.
> Having the right asset allocation can help improve your returns and help you feel better about your investments.
> Choosing the right asset allocation is mainly about choosing the right risk level, and should be driven by your investing time horizon and your risk appetite.

Some examples of self-care include meditation, exfoliation, and asset allocation. —Napkin Finance ☺

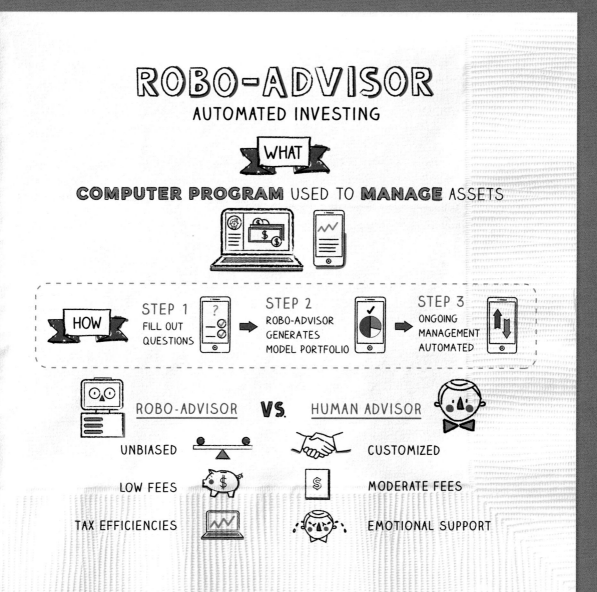

ROBO-ADVISOR
AUTOMATED INVESTING

WHAT

COMPUTER PROGRAM USED TO **MANAGE** ASSETS

HOW

STEP 1
FILL OUT
QUESTIONS

→

STEP 2
ROBO-ADVISOR
GENERATES
MODEL PORTFOLIO

→

STEP 3
ONGOING
MANAGEMENT
AUTOMATED

ROBO-ADVISOR **VS.** HUMAN ADVISOR

UNBIASED

LOW FEES

TAX EFFICIENCIES

CUSTOMIZED

MODERATE FEES

EMOTIONAL SUPPORT

Robo-Advisor

A robo-advisor is an investment management company that uses a computer program, instead of a live human, to manage assets.

Start-ups, such as Betterment and Wealthfront, invented the concept of robo-advising. But it's been so successful that now financial giants such as Charles Schwab, Fidelity, and Vanguard have gotten in on the action.

How It Works

Step 1: You create an account online with a robo-advisor firm and fund your account.

Step 2: You answer a few basic questions about your investment goals, time horizon, and risk tolerance.

Step 3: Using your answers, the robo-advisor creates a portfolio of investments. Often, robo-advisors have a few different preset investment strategies and portfolios to work with.

Step 4: The robo-advisor invests your funds in the chosen portfolio.

Step 5: The robo-advisor monitors your portfolio, and may make trades in response to market movements, your chosen strategy, or changes in your risk profile.

Trade-Offs

Compared with using a traditional, human financial advisor, using a robo-advisor can come with some important distinctions.

	Robo-advisor	Traditional advisor
Fees	Typically low, such as 0.25% per year.	Can be moderate to high, such as 1% per year.
Quality of advice	Unbiased and objective.	Customized and subjective.
Investment options	Limited—but often limited to solid choices.	Range and quality vary with the advisor.
Bonus	Many use special trading strategies to minimize the taxes you pay on your investing gains.	If you're anxious about your investments, you have someone you know and trust to talk to.
May be best if	Your needs are fairly simple and you feel comfortable with investing.	Your needs are more complex and you'd like a hand to hold.

Fun Facts

› Assets managed by robo-advisors have exploded, from $0 in 2008, to $1 billion in 2012, to $200 billion in 2017, to a projected $16 trillion by 2025.

› Some robo-advisors have started offering clients phone access to financial planners (computers still handle the investing decisions), because even millennials sometimes want to interact with an actual human.

Key Takeaways

› A robo-advisor is an investment manager that uses automation to manage funds.

> › Robo-advisors may have a number of preset portfolios or strategies that they can choose from, to match a user's risk profile.
> › Compared with human advisors, robo-advisors are typically cheaper, but offer less emotional support.

Robo-advisors are great for if you want to get financial advice without having to put on pants. —Napkin Finance ☺

Chapter Quiz

1. Investing is:

   a. Basically gambling, but more socially acceptable.
   b. A guaranteed way to join the 1%.
   c. Putting two dollar bills into a jar and hoping they make baby dollars.
   d. A way of personally sharing in the growth of the broader economy.

2. True or false: Savings accounts make great long-term investments because they provide excellent growth.

   ○ True   ○ False

3. The main investing asset classes are:

   a. Stocks, funds, shares, and bonds.
   b. Stocks, bonds, cash, and alternatives.
   c. Cash under your mattress, coins in your old sock, and gold bars you bury in the backyard.
   d. Khloé, Kim, Kourtney, Kendall, and Kylie.

4. **A stock is:**
   a. A fractional piece of ownership in a company.
   b. The name of the old sock where you keep all your share certificates.
   c. An ingredient in soup.
   d. A type of account where you can hold investments tax-free.

5. **Alternative investments can include all of the following except:**
   a. Hedge funds.
   b. Jewelry.
   c. Stocks.
   d. Old Nirvana memorabilia.

6. **Diversification is:**
   a. A strategy of buying and selling throughout the trading day to maximize your gains.
   b. A strategy of spreading your money around with lots of different types of investments.
   c. A strategy for minimizing the taxes you pay on your investments.
   d. What was lacking in the sitcom *Friends*.

7. **True or false: Diversification can reduce the risk of your portfolio and smooth your returns.**
   ○ True   ○ False

8. **Ways to diversify include all of the following except:**
   a. Holding investments from different countries.
   b. Holding investments in different industries.
   c. Investing in some small companies and some large companies.
   d. Investing in companies with names that start with different letters.

9. **True or false: Investments that return more are also generally lower risk.**

   ○ True   ○ False

10. **The main way of thinking about risk is in terms of how much an investment swings in price. That's called:**

    a. Motility.
    b. Hypermobility.
    c. Volatility.
    d. Fertility.

11. **One very risky type of investment is:**

    a. Certificates of deposit.
    b. Cryptocurrency.
    c. Bonds.
    d. Preferred stocks.

12. **One very safe type of investment is:**

    a. Vintage motorcycles.
    b. Junk bonds.
    c. MoviePass stock.
    d. Savings accounts.

13. **Asset allocation describes:**

    a. The types of investments you own in percentage terms.
    b. Which investments you hold in domestic accounts and which you hold in offshore accounts.
    c. Your best features for your dating profile.
    d. A new type of cosmetic surgery.

14. **The right asset allocation for you is mainly determined by:**

    a. How much money you have and how lucky you're feeling.
    b. Your biological age minus your actual level of maturity.
    c. Your time horizon and your personal risk appetite.
    d. How many followers you have on Instagram.

15. **True or false: You can come up with a decent starting point for your asset allocation using just your age.**

    ○ True   ○ False

16. **Robo-advisors are:**

    a. Algorithms that pick winning stocks.

    b. Companies that can manage your investments using automation.

    c. Digital pets that you can buy and dress up in the robo-advisor app.

    d. The alien robot race that colonized Earth 5 million years ago.

17. **The pros of robo-advisors include all of the following, except:**

    a. Low fees.

    b. Unbiased advice.

    c. Potential tax minimization.

    d. Wide menu of investment options.

18. **One of the biggest advantages of human advisors over robo-advisors is:**

    a. Stronger regulatory protections.

    b. You can literally cry on their shoulder if your investments tank.

    c. Lower fees.

    d. A better investing track record.

Answers

1. d	**6.** b	**11.** b	**16.** b
2. f	**7.** t	**12.** d	**17.** d
3. b	**8.** d	**13.** a	**18.** b
4. a	**9.** f	**14.** c	
5. c	**10.** c	**15.** t	

4

Paying Your Dues

COLLEGE

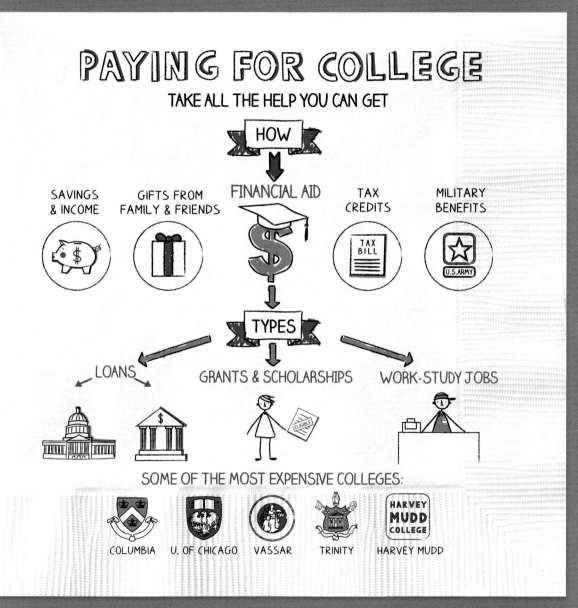

Paying for College

It takes more than hard work to make it through college; it also takes buckets and buckets of cash. More specifically, it costs about $26,000 on average per year, including room, board, and books, at an in-state public college. The average cost at private colleges is more than twice that—$53,000 per year.

Those prices have been increasing by about 6% per year. At that rate, in twenty years a degree could easily cost more than $500,000.

Follow the Money

If you don't have a wealthy great-aunt to bankroll your higher education, how do you find the money? The average student's funding sources look like this:

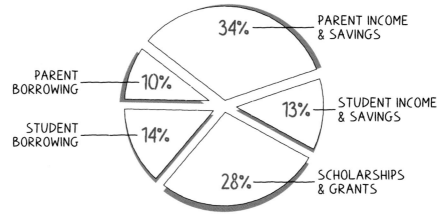

34% — PARENT INCOME & SAVINGS

PARENT BORROWING — 10%

STUDENT BORROWING — 14%

13% — STUDENT INCOME & SAVINGS

28% — SCHOLARSHIPS & GRANTS

Percentages do not sum to 100 due to rounding.

Ways to Pay

Here's a basic rundown of the options:

> *Income and savings*—chances are both you and your parents will need to contribute pretty heavily.

> *Scholarships and grants*—aka *free money*! Your school's financial aid office can help you find opportunities, but you should also do your own research to find private scholarships.

> *Work-study jobs*—one perk is that these jobs don't affect your financial aid eligibility (unlike other jobs).

> *Federal loans*—money you borrow from the government, usually at a low interest rate. These loans come with certain protections if you face financial hardship when it's time to repay. Examples include Direct Subsidized Loans and Direct Unsubsidized Loans.

> *Private loans*—money you borrow from a private entity, usually at a higher rate and with fewer protections. You'll also generally need your parents to cosign.

> *Tax credits*—you may be able to claim a tax credit for part of what you spend on tuition and other expenses.

> *Military service*—if you serve in the military for a certain length of time before attending college, you may qualify for education benefits.

"An investment in knowledge pays the best interest."

—BENJAMIN FRANKLIN, FOUNDING FATHER

Fun Facts

> There are actual scholarships available for vegetarians, for being left-handed, for being tall (or short), and for people with the last name Zolp.
> Prices at private colleges have been rising at more than twice the rate of inflation in recent years.

Key Takeaways

> College is incredibly expensive.
> Most families use a combination of savings, income, grants, scholarships, and loans to afford it.

A college education is important so you'll be able to get a good job to pay for your college education. —Napkin Finance ☺

Student Loans

A student loan can be any kind of borrowed money that's used to pay for education. Although the name might imply that the loans are only provided to students themselves, parents may also take out loans to help pay for their kids' education.

Types

There are two main types of student loans: federal loans and private loans. Federal loans are made by the federal government, and come in a few varieties:

> Direct subsidized federal loans—low-interest-rate loans to students who demonstrate financial need.
> > Interest doesn't accrue on these loans while you're still in school.

STUDENT LOANS

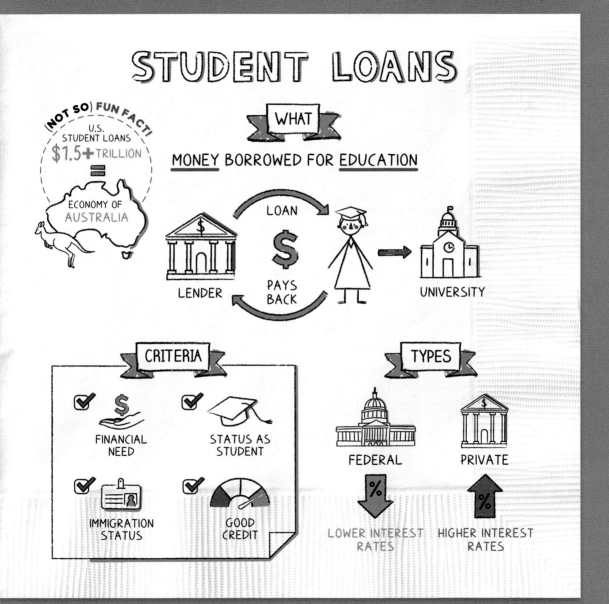

(NOT SO) FUN FACT!

U.S. STUDENT LOANS
$1.5+ TRILLION
=
ECONOMY OF AUSTRALIA

WHAT

MONEY BORROWED FOR EDUCATION

LOAN

$

PAYS BACK

LENDER

UNIVERSITY

CRITERIA

FINANCIAL NEED

STATUS AS STUDENT

IMMIGRATION STATUS

GOOD CREDIT

TYPES

FEDERAL

PRIVATE

LOWER INTEREST RATES

HIGHER INTEREST RATES

- Direct unsubsidized federal loans—low-interest-rate loans to students who don't necessarily demonstrate financial need.
  - Interest does accrue on these while you're still in school.
- Parent PLUS loans—moderate-rate loans to parents, who have to pass a credit check in order to qualify.
  - Parents have to start making payments on the loans while their child is still in school.
- Federal Perkins loans—low-interest loans to students with extreme financial need.
  - This program expired in 2017, but could be reauthorized.

In contrast, private loans are generally made by private financial services companies, such as banks, credit unions, and Sallie Mae. Terms of private loans depend on the lender.

How to Qualify

Depending on the lender or type of loan, you may need to show:

- Financial need.
- Status as at least a part-time student.
- Citizenship or immigration status.
- A good credit history.

Good to Know

Be careful when it comes to private loans, as they are typically more expensive than federal loans and are less forgiving if you have trouble meeting payments later in life.

Fun Facts

› At more than $1.5 trillion, if Americans' student loans were a country, they would be the thirteenth-largest economy in the world (roughly the size of Australia).

› More than half of student-loan borrowers wrongly assume their payments will be based on their income, and almost 10% wrongly believe they won't have to pay off their loans if they can't find a job. (Correct answers: Unless you make an alternate arrangement, payments are based on how much you borrowed, how long you have to pay the loan back, and the interest rate. And yes, you still have to pay your loans back if you can't find a job.)

Key Takeaways

› Student loans are funds borrowed to pay for education.

› The main types are federal loans and private loans. Federal loans are typically less expensive and come with extra protections for borrowers.

› Depending on the type of loan, you may need to demonstrate financial need, creditworthiness, your status as a student, and your immigration status in order to qualify for a loan.

Anti-aging hack: Feel ten years younger by still having student loans to pay off.
—Napkin Finance ☺

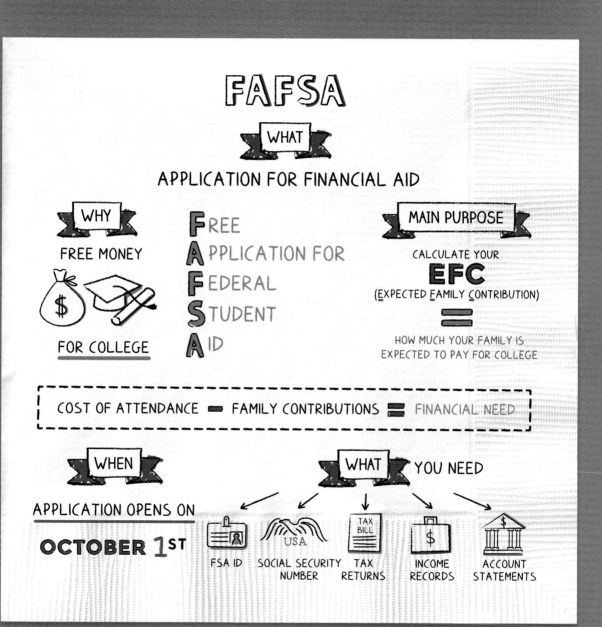

FAFSA

The Free Application for Federal Student Aid, or FAFSA, is a form that students fill out annually as part of the financial aid process.

How It Works

Step 1: Apply for a Federal Student Aid ID and password.

Step 2: Gather all the documents you'll need and wait until filing opens (on October 1 of the year before the school year you're applying for).

Step 3: Fill out the form at the official FAFSA website: studentaid.ed.gov.

Step 4: After you've completed the form, look at your Student Aid Report. That's a breakdown of the information you entered, and shows your "Expected Family Contribution"—the amount that your family is considered able to pay.

Step 5: Your school (or schools, if you're in application mode) receive your financial information through the FAFSA. For each school, the cost of attendance minus your Expected Family Contribution equals the amount of need-based aid you're eligible for.

Step 6: Your school or schools send out their financial aid letters—often in March or April.

Why Important

More than $120 billion in federal aid is awarded each year. Many states and schools also use your FAFSA information in awarding their own aid, such as school-specific scholarships.

What You Need

To fill out the form, you typically need:

> › Your Social Security number.
> › Your most recent tax returns (or your parents' returns, if you're twenty-four or under or a dependent).
> › Any bank or brokerage statements.
> › Records for any other types of income.

> *"It's one thing to make financial aid available to students so they can attend college. It's another thing to design forms that students can actually fill out."*
>
> —CASS SUNSTEIN, LEGAL SCHOLAR

Fun Facts

> › One common FAFSA mistake is parents accidentally entering their own information instead of their kids'.
> › It's called the "Free" application for aid because it's free, but some copycat private websites may still try to get you to file with them for a fee. (Hint: You never have to enter credit card information to fill out the real FAFSA.)

Key Takeaways

> › FAFSA is a form you fill out to access financial aid.
> › Filling out the FAFSA on time can help you qualify for several types of aid, including need-based and merit-based aid, and federal, state, and school-specific aid.

FAFSA be like "we see your parents got extra guacamole at lunch . . . you must not need any aid." —Napkin Finance ☺

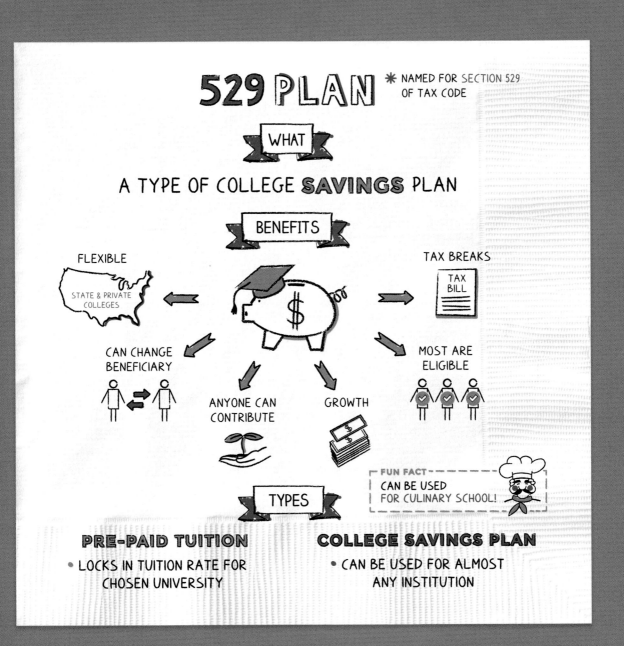

529 Plan

A 529 plan is a tax-advantaged college savings account sponsored by a state government or education institution. The plans are kind of like 401(k)s for college funds. (The name comes from the section of the tax code that authorizes the accounts.)

Types

There are two types of 529 plans:

› Savings plans, which let you build up assets that you can use toward almost any U.S. college
› Pre-paid tuition plans, which can let parents pay today's tuition rates for a child's future education (but may limit where a child can go to school)

Not surprisingly, the more flexible savings plans tend to be more popular.

Benefits

529s can offer several significant advantages, including:

› Tax breaks—Your money can grow tax-free in a 529 account and be withdrawn tax-free, as long as you use funds for qualifying expenses. Depending on which state's plan you choose and what state you live in, you may also get a state tax deduction on contributions.
› Potential growth—You typically have a number of investment options to choose from in a 529, so your money can grow.
› No restrictions on who can contribute—Grandma's birthday check can go straight into the 529.

- › Few restrictions on eligibility—Even high-income families can use the plans.
- › Flexibility—You can invest in any state's 529 program. And funds from any state's plan can be used at any of more than six thousand schools.
- › Ability to change beneficiary—If a child (or other beneficiary) doesn't end up going to college, you can change the beneficiary to anyone else (including yourself).

Drawbacks

The only significant drawback is that the plans place restrictions on withdrawals. If you withdraw money for noneducational expenses you'll typically pay a 10% penalty, plus income taxes on any withdrawn earnings.

Fun Facts

- › 529 assets can be used to pay for vocational school—including some culinary, acting, and massage-therapy schools (but not any clown colleges).
- › You can also use the assets at a handful of schools abroad, including for a destination education at some schools in the Cayman Islands, St. Maarten, and St. John.
- › Parents tend to save more money toward boys' college educations than toward girls' college funds.

Key Takeaways

- › 529 plans can help families save for college.
- › More popular 529 savings accounts are like 401(k)s for college.
  529 pre-paid tuition plans let parents pay tuition now for their kids' future education.

> › The benefits of 529 plans include tax breaks, flexibility, and the ability to change an account's beneficiary.

The road to college isn't paved with gold, but it is paved with tax breaks if you have a 529 plan. —Napkin Finance ☺

Paying Off Student Loans

It might seem like there's only one way to pay down your student loans (namely: slowly, painfully, and for the rest of your life). But there are actually a few different ways you may be able to structure your payments, depending on whether you want to pay off your loans ASAP or whether you need more time.

The Standard Option

Your federal loans will default to a ten-year repayment schedule, with equal payments. That's great if you're making grown-up money as soon as you graduate, but some find it hard to make payments in the first few years.

With private loans, you probably agreed to a loan term and payment schedule when you took out the loan. These terms can vary widely based on the lender and based on the details of your situation (such as how much you're borrowing and whether a parent is cosigning).

Pay Faster

If you can afford to, consider making more than the minimum monthly payment on your loans (whether federal or private), because you'll save money on interest by doing so.

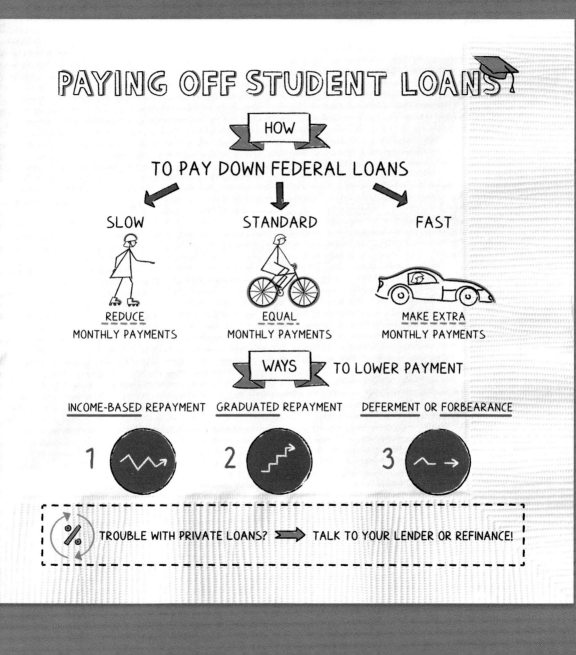

If you have multiple loans, consider paying anything extra toward the loan with the highest interest rate first (probably any private loans you have).

Pay Slower

If you're having trouble making your payments, your options depend on what type of loans you have. For federal loans, they include:

> › Income-based or income-contingent repayment—Payments will be based on your income. If your salary goes up, you'll pay down your loans faster, but if not, you won't drown in your bills.
>
> › Graduated repayment or extended graduated repayment—With these plans your payments start low, then slowly increase according to a preset schedule.
>
> › Deferment or forbearance—Either can give you a temporary break from payments, but you must apply and meet eligibility requirements. (And neither dings your credit score—so they're much better options than simply skipping a payment.)

If you work in public service, you could even qualify for outright forgiveness of your federal loans after a certain number of years.

If you're struggling with your private loans, you may be able to talk to your lender to get a temporary break or to adjust your payment terms. If not, your main option will be to try to refinance your loans to:

> › A lower interest rate, which could save you money in total and lower your monthly bill.

> A longer payment term, which will increase your total but can lower what you pay each month.

Fun Facts

> Want to pay off your loans fast? Try becoming a software developer, which typically ranks as a top-paying career option for new grads.
> A common myth is that student loans can never be discharged in bankruptcy. In fact, about 40% of bankruptcy filers who ask to have their loans discharged succeed (though you have to meet strict eligibility requirements).
> Barack and Michelle Obama didn't finish paying off their student loans until they were in their forties.

Key Takeaways

> Your student loans will default to a certain payment structure—such as ten years of equal payments for federal loans.
> If you can afford to, paying extra toward your loans can save you money in interest.
> There are several options that can give you breathing room from your federal loans.
> Private loans typically don't offer as many payment choices, but refinancing could reduce your interest rate or lower your monthly payments.

Whoever said diamonds are a girl's best friend obviously never experienced the high of paying off their student loans. —Napkin Finance ☺

Chapter Quiz

1. **The main sources of funds for college include all of the following except:**

   a. Savings and income.
   b. Scholarships and grants.
   c. Federal and private loans.
   d. Kidnapping a trust-fund baby.

2. **True or false: The largest source of funds for the average college student is loans.**

   ○ True   ○ False

3. **True or false: Your college financial aid office can refer you to all the grants and scholarships you should apply for.**

   ○ True   ○ False

4. **Types of student loans include:**

   a. Secured and unsecured.
   b. Federal and private.
   c. Raw and toasted.
   d. Hall and Oates.

5. **Criteria lenders may evaluate when deciding whether or not to offer you a student loan can include:**

   a. Your family's assets and income.
   b. Your declared major.
   c. Your zodiac sign.
   d. Your number of Instagram followers.

6. **True or false: Private loans can come with different—and less favorable—terms than federal loans.**

    ○ True   ○ False

7. **FAFSA is:**
    a. A popular drink in Mexico.
    b. A required form you have to fill out before you can enroll at college.
    c. A form for financial aid that you should fill out even though it's optional.
    d. The new Zika.

8. **The main point of the FAFSA form is:**
    a. To prove your family can afford the cost of college.
    b. To prove you aren't an AI robot.
    c. To assess whether you want to go to college badly enough to make it through a mind-numbing form.
    d. To calculate how much money your family should be expected to contribute to your education in a given year.

9. **True or false: FAFSA is only used in awarding federal aid.**

    ○ True   ○ False

10. **The two main types of 529 plans are:**
    a. Undergrad and graduate plans.
    b. Savings and pre-paid tuition plans.
    c. Private and federal plans.
    d. Diet plans and exercise plans.

11. **The benefits of 529 plans include all of the following except:**

    a. A guaranteed employer match.
    b. Potential tax breaks.
    c. A chance to grow your money by investing it.
    d. The ability to change an account's beneficiary.

12. **True or false: You can set up a 529 plan for yourself.**

    ○ True   ○ False

13. **True or false: You can use a 529 plan to pay for vocational school, such as cooking or acting school.**

    ○ True   ○ False

14. **If you're having trouble meeting your student loan payments, you should:**

    a. Ignore the bills, because they're just pieces of paper and life is short.
    b. Move to Peru.
    c. Work with your lender to come up with a more manageable payment schedule.
    d. Build a time machine, go back in time, and go to state school instead.

15. **If you're having trouble making payments on your federal student loans, your options may include all of the following except:**

    a. Deferment or forbearance.
    b. Basing payments on your income.
    c. Switching to a graduated repayment schedule.
    d. Declaring thumb war.

16. True or false: Student loans can never be discharged in bankruptcy.

○ True   ○ False

Answers

1. d	**5.** a	**9.** f	**13.** t
2. f	**6.** t	**10.** b	**14.** c
3. f	**7.** c	**11.** a	**15.** d
4. b	**8.** d	**12.** t	**16.** f

5

Into the Sunset

RETIREMENT

PAYING FOR RETIREMENT

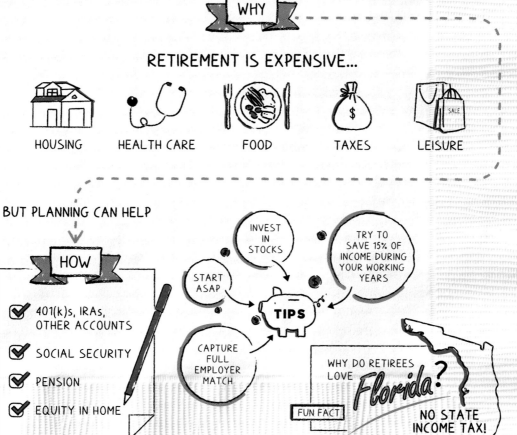

WHY

RETIREMENT IS EXPENSIVE...

HOUSING   HEALTH CARE   FOOD   TAXES   LEISURE

BUT PLANNING CAN HELP

HOW

- ✓ 401(k)s, IRAs, OTHER ACCOUNTS
- ✓ SOCIAL SECURITY
- ✓ PENSION
- ✓ EQUITY IN HOME

INVEST IN STOCKS

TRY TO SAVE 15% OF INCOME DURING YOUR WORKING YEARS

START ASAP

TIPS

CAPTURE FULL EMPLOYER MATCH

WHY DO RETIREES LOVE Florida?

FUN FACT

NO STATE INCOME TAX!

Paying for Retirement

Retirement may seem like an abstract, far-off goal (unless you're already independently wealthy or a 401(k) ninja, in which case—respect). But you'll never drink mai tais on the beach in your seventies unless you start saving money now.

Why

Retirement is expensive. Your costs in retirement will probably include:

- › Housing.
- › Health care.
- › Food.
- › Taxes.
- › Leisure.

How

Your income and assets in retirement may include:

- › Investment and savings accounts—including what you've saved in retirement accounts.
- › Social Security—which is paid by the government.
- › Traditional pension—if you worked for an employer that provides one.
- › Your house—if you own your home.

What You Can Do

Paying into Social Security generally happens automatically when you work. Unfortunately, you probably don't have any control over whether your employer offers a traditional pension.

The main thing you can do to plan for your retirement is to save—particularly in a tax-advantaged retirement account where your money can grow. The main types of accounts include:

› 401(k)s—tax-deferred accounts offered by many employers. (Employees of nonprofits and public-school systems may have 403(b)s instead.)
› Individual Retirement Accounts (IRAs)—tax-deferred accounts you can open on your own, with a financial institution.
› Roth 401(k)s and Roth IRAs—accounts similar to their non-Roth counterparts, but which let you contribute after-tax dollars and take withdrawals tax-free in retirement.

Tips

Saving enough for retirement takes some planning and effort. Many experts recommend that you:

› Start ASAP, such as with your first job that offers a retirement savings plan. (Or, open an IRA on your own.)
› Try to save 15% of your annual income each year while you're working.
› Invest heavily in stocks while you're young, since they generally grow your money faster over the long term.

"Retirement is like a long vacation in Las Vegas. The goal is to enjoy it to the fullest, but not so fully that you run out of money."
—JONATHAN CLEMENTS, AUTHOR

> Invest enough in your 401(k) or other workplace plan to capture the full amount of any match your employer offers.

Fun Facts

> Why do retirees love Florida so much? It's not just the sunshine and beaches—it's also one of the seven states with no personal income tax.
> The country with the youngest retirement age is the United Arab Emirates, where citizens become eligible for pensions and retirement benefits at forty-nine (expats have to wait until they're sixty-five).

Key Takeaways

> Retirement is expensive, so you need to start saving for it while you're young.
> Tax-advantaged retirement accounts, such as 401(k)s and IRAs, are the best retirement savings options for many people.
> Saving 15% of your income and investing heavily in stocks while you're young can help you get there.

Retirement is like making a soufflé: you must plan for it in advance.
—Napkin Finance ☺

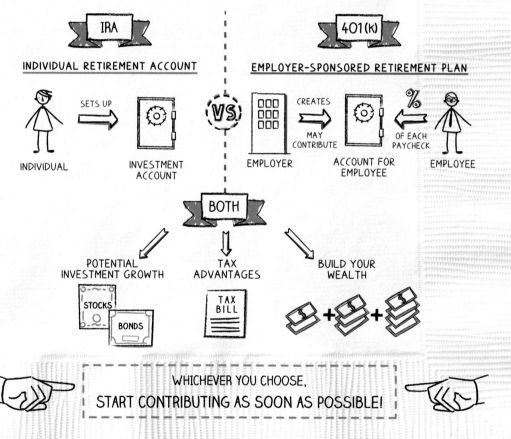

IRA vs. 401(k)

IRAs and 401(k)s are two popular types of retirement savings accounts. Most people who work in the private sector have at least one of these accounts (government employees often have different options), and many people own several different retirement accounts.

Differences

Although they both serve the same purpose, the accounts have some important distinctions:

	IRAs	401(k)s
How do you open an account?	Open an account with a financial institution and deposit some money.	Your employer must sponsor an account, and you sign up through HR.
How do you contribute?	Send money to your account.	Set up automatic payroll deductions.
When can I use the money?	Not until age 59.5, other than a few exceptions, such as for financial hardship.	Not until age 59.5, other than a few exceptions, such as for financial hardship.
Perks	Lots of choices for investment options. Easy to consolidate accounts or move them to a new financial institution.	Free money! Many employers match your contributions up to a certain amount.

Benefits

Both types of accounts can provide great perks, including:

› Potential growth—both IRAs and 401(k)s typically offer a range of investment options you can choose from, so your money grows over time.
› Tax advantages—both types of accounts let you avoid paying taxes on your money's growth while it's in the account.
› Chance to build your wealth—by contributing regularly and letting your money grow, you can use either account type to meet your retirement goals.

Fun Facts

› What's the FIRE community? No, it's not a Burning Man camp—it's "Financial Independence, Retire Early," a movement of millennials obsessed with aggressively saving money, so that they can retire early.
› The average balance in a 401(k) is just over $100,000, but it is possible to become a "401(k) millionaire"—i.e., someone with a balance in the seven digits. #goals

Key Takeaways

› IRAs and 401(k)s are the two main types of retirement savings accounts.
› The main difference is that 401(k)s must be sponsored by an employer, while you can set up an IRA on your own.
› Either, or both, can be a great option for retirement savings.

IRAs and 401(k)s can make you rich enough that your grandchildren will want to stay in touch with you. —Napkin Finance ☺

Social Security

Social Security is a government program that pays money out to people if they become disabled, reach retirement age, or meet certain other eligibility requirements. It's essentially a nationwide safety net.

How It Works

Step 1: You contribute while you're in the workforce. If you're an employee, you'll see a big chunk of earnings taken out of your paychecks for FICA (almost 8% for most people, but more for high earners). Those are your contributions to Social Security and Medicare.

Step 2: The more money you earn during your career, the more you pay into the system and the better your future benefits should be.

Step 3: Once you turn sixty-two you're eligible to start taking benefits, though it can make sense to wait until age seventy if you can because you'll receive a larger monthly benefit if you do. Once you start taking benefits, you'll generally receive a check from the government every month for the rest of your life.

What It Covers

Although its best-known benefits are probably those retirement checks, Social Security pays for some other important programs, including:

› Disability benefits—You can receive benefits if you become disabled.
› Benefits for survivors—If the family breadwinner dies, his or her spouse or children may be eligible for benefits.

> › Medicare—Your FICA contributions also fund Medicare, the government-provided health insurance plan that covers older people.

What It Is and What It Isn't

Think of Social Security as a little extra cash that will be nice to have, but not as something that's going to bankroll your globe-trotting golden years. The program is politically controversial—with liberals typically preferring a strong Social Security safety net and conservatives advocating for smaller benefits and lower taxes. And the program has perennial funding problems. It's not 100% guaranteed that it will be there when you retire.

Fun Facts

› What you pay into Social Security today goes to pay today's benefits to some retiree somewhere (which means your future benefits will have to be funded by the workforce of the next generation). So if we're destined for a *Handmaid's Tale*–type fertility apocalypse, good luck claiming your benefits.

› You can't receive Social Security if you're in prison.

› The Netherlands has, arguably, the world's best pension system, where almost all workers are covered and can expect to receive about 70% of their annual salary from their working years in retirement.

Key Takeaways

› Social Security is a government safety net that pays benefits to the elderly, the disabled, and survivors.

› To receive Social Security benefits in retirement, you need to pay into the system during your working years.

> Social Security can add some padding to your retirement income, but don't count on it to be your sole source of income.

Silly rabbit, Social Security is for people at least sixty-two. —Napkin Finance ☺

Estate Planning

Estate planning is the process of figuring out what will happen to your stuff after you die. It's coming up with a plan for your assets, then writing your plan down in a way that's legally valid (and that a court would recognize as enforceable).

Why Important

Having an estate plan can be an important way to:

> *I made my money the old-fashioned way. I was very nice to a wealthy relative right before he died."*
> —MALCOLM FORBES, PUBLISHER

› Provide for your family if something should happen to you.
› Transfer assets to your survivors faster— by hopefully skipping a trip through the court system.
› Reduce taxes. If you're wealthy, there may be legal strategies you can use to lower taxes on your assets after you die.
› Plan for disabilities. An estate plan typically also includes documents that specify your wishes if you become unable to make decisions on your own behalf.

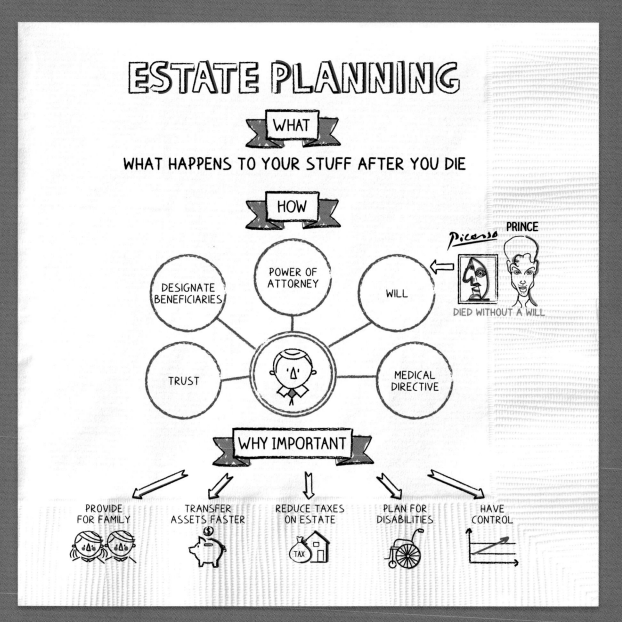

> Have control. Maybe you want to make sure that your best friend inherits some prized possession, or maybe you want to make sure that your ex-spouse doesn't. Either way, with an estate plan, you get to decide.

What

An estate plan is basically a collection of documents, and might include the following:

> Will—your will can specify who gets which of your stuff and who should take care of your kids (or pet turtle).

> Health-care directive or power of attorney—these may dictate who is authorized to make decisions for you, if you can't make them for yourself.

> Trust—if you're wealthy or have a more complicated financial situation, a trust might make sense for some of your assets.

> Beneficiary designations—some financial accounts let you specify in your paperwork who should receive the account if you pass away. (These designations are important because they can trump what you say in your will.)

> *"Death is not the end. There remains the litigation over the estate."*
> —AMBROSE BIERCE, WRITER

Who Needs It

Estate planning isn't just for the rich. If you have kids and you don't have a will, it could be up to the courts to decide who takes care of them if you die. If you're in a relationship but not married, your partner could get left out in the cold if something happened to you.

Fun Facts

› Prince and Pablo Picasso both died without wills.

› Abraham Lincoln also died without a will, even though he was a lawyer (and president).

› Although Jimi Hendrix died in 1970, legal battles within his family over his estate have continued until recent years because he didn't leave a will.

Key Takeaways

› Estate planning is the process of deciding on and documenting a plan for what will happen to your things after you die.

› Having an estate plan is extremely important if you have dependents, but it can be useful for anyone to make sure their wishes are followed after they pass away.

Probably best if turkeys do their estate planning before Thanksgiving.
—Napkin Finance ☺

Chapter Quiz

1. You should start saving for retirement:

a. As soon as you get your driver's license.

b. One year after your last Coachella.

c. By the time you turn fifty.

d. By the time you get your first job that offers a retirement savings plan.

2. **Your sources of income in retirement should probably include:**
   a. Dividends on your Bitcoin holdings.
   b. Your earnings as a social media influencer.
   c. Social Security and your investment accounts.
   d. Your reverse mortgage.

3. **The main thing you can do to boost your chance of a comfy retirement is to:**
   a. Save as much as you can during your working years.
   b. Invest your retirement savings mainly in safe options such as bonds and savings accounts.
   c. Suck up to rich relatives.
   d. Buy a recliner.

4. **A solid savings rate to aim for with your retirement savings is:**
   a. 10% of your after-tax profits.
   b. 20% of your investment gains.
   c. 15% of your income.
   d. 30% of your kombucha and cold-brew expenses.

5. **The two main types of retirement accounts are:**
   a. IRA and GLASS accounts.
   b. IRAs and 401(k)s.
   c. Guaranteed and non-guaranteed accounts.
   d. Subsidized and unsubsidized accounts.

6. **Who can contribute to a 401(k)?**
   a. You and your employer.
   b. You and the federal government.
   c. Your parents and your stepparents.
   d. Anyone who's already finished four 10ks.

7. **The benefits of 401(k)s and IRAs include:**

   a. TSA pre-check when you travel.
   b. Back rubs on your birthday.
   c. Flexible withdrawals.
   d. Tax advantages and compound growth.

8. **True or false: You can open a 401(k) on your own.**

   ○ True   ○ False

9. **Social Security is:**

   a. A movie starring Liam Neeson.
   b. A guarantee of a cushy retirement.
   c. A federal safety net that pays benefits to the elderly and disabled.
   d. The name of Franklin D. Roosevelt's cat.

10. **FICA is:**

    a. A type of wood.
    b. A credit-reporting bureau.
    c. This guy who keeps siphoning money from your paycheck.
    d. The federal payroll tax that funds Social Security.

11. **True or false: The more money you earn, the better your Social Security benefits should be.**

    ○ True   ○ False

12. **You can claim Social Security:**

    a. At sixty-two, though you can boost your benefits by waiting until age seventy.
    b. As long as you've been paying into the system for at least five years.
    c. As soon as you retire, no matter your age.
    d. After your third colonoscopy.

13. **Estate planning is for:**
    a. Old rich people.
    b. Basically anyone.
    c. No one, because scientists are really close to cracking this whole mortality thing.
    d. Batman.

14. **The benefits of estate planning can include all of the following except:**
    a. Reducing taxes.
    b. Letting you rank your friends and family according to how much you love them, and giving everything to the ones at the top of the list and nothing to the ones at the bottom.
    c. Increasing the size of your estate.
    d. Making sure that your kids or other dependents will be taken care of if something happens to you.

15. **Your estate plan may include:**
    a. Your remaining Social Security payments.
    b. Your detailed list of complaints about each family member.
    c. Your Internet search history.
    d. Your will and your beneficiary designations.

Answers

1. d	**5.** b	**9.** c	**13.** b
2. c	**6.** a	**10.** d	**14.** c
3. a	**7.** d	**11.** t	**15.** d
4. c	**8.** f	**12.** a	

6

A Wild Ride

THE STOCK MARKET

Stocks

We introduced stocks in chapter 3. Stocks are pieces of ownership in companies. If you bought one stock of, say, Amazon, and Amazon had one million shares in total, then you would own one-millionth of the company. (In reality, it has more like 500 million shares.)

Why Invest in Stocks

People invest in stocks because they hope to earn a better return on their money than they could with a safer alternative, such as a savings account. Investors earn returns on stocks in two main ways:

› Price gains—If you buy a stock when the share price is $100, it rises to $150, and then you sell it, then you've made a 50% profit.
› Dividends—Some companies pay out a portion of profits to their shareholders in the form of cash dividends. If you own a stock with a price of $100 and it pays out $2 four times a year, you're earning about 8% per year.

Why Stock Prices Change

You can think of the stock market as one giant auction, except the auction never ends. Each trading day, shares of Amazon (and every other publicly traded company: see IPO section later in this chapter) are potentially up for sale, and prospective buyers and sellers put out bids for what they're willing to pay or receive for the shares.

The interplay between buyers and sellers is what drives the stock price. If one group of investors think Amazon stock is actually worth $3,000, then they'll probably be willing to buy it at $2,000. If another group of investors think the stock is only worth $1,500, they'll probably be willing to sell it at $2,000.

How do investors come up with their opinions of what the stock is worth? People disagree about the best way to figure out a stock's value, but one of the most common ways is to estimate the company's future profits, and then decide how much you're willing to pay for those profits. If negative developments about the company come out in the media, investors will lower their estimate for future profits, and the stock price will fall. If good news comes out, the reverse typically happens.

Key Terms

Here are some must-know terms about stocks:

> Dividend: What a company pays out, periodically, to shareholders. (Not all companies pay dividends. Younger companies often prefer to hold on to their cash so that they can use it to keep growing their businesses.)

> Earnings per share: The company's total profits for a given period, divided by the number of shares. It's an estimate of what portion of profits each shareholder is "entitled to" (in theory—investors don't actually get paid this amount).

> Share price: The price the stock is currently trading for in the market.

> Stocks, shares, and equities: These words all mean the same thing.

> Ticker symbol: A short string of letters that identifies a given stock. If you wanted to trade Amazon's stock, you would look up its ticker, AMZN, with your broker.

Fun Facts

> Some companies get cheeky with their ticker symbols, like Harley-Davidson (HOG), mattress company Sealy (ZZ), and Heineken (HEINY).

> A "fat finger" error is when a trader accidentally adds extra digits to a trade—like the time a Lehman Brothers trader entered a stock order for £300 million instead of £3 million, and briefly wiped out about £30 billion in value from the London Stock Exchange.

Key Takeaways

> Stocks are fractional shares of ownership in companies.
> Investors earn money on stocks through dividends and price gains.
> Stock prices are largely driven by investors' expectations as to a company's future profits.

When ending a call about your stocks with your broker, be sure you don't confuse "bye-bye" with "buy-buy!" —Napkin Finance ☺

Stock Market

The stock market is the collection of physical and electronic markets where buyers and sellers come together to trade shares. Most (though not all) of the world's stock trading happens through stock exchanges. If the stock market is like one giant auction, then stock exchanges are a bit like individual auction houses.

How Exchanges Work

The main stock exchanges in the U.S. are:

> The New York Stock Exchange (NYSE)—which has a physical trading floor, but also handles electronic orders.
> The Nasdaq—which is an all-electronic exchange.

Their main roles are to:

> › Match buyers and sellers.
> › Keep trade traffic flowing.
> › Track and report data on trades, so investors can see what the market is doing.

Investors can only trade stocks that are "listed" on a given exchange with that exchange. But most individual investors (like you) don't trade directly with the exchange. Instead, you'd set up an account with a broker, which handles the actual mechanics of trading for you.

What Makes the Stock Market Move

The stock market is really the sum of all individual stocks. When an individual stock moves—because, say, investors are estimating higher or lower profits—the market as a whole moves a tiny bit (think fractions of fractions of a percent).

But often lots of stocks move up and down together because of big-picture stuff that's happening in the economy. For some of those big-picture things that tend to move the market, see the table on the facing page.

Fun Facts

> › Wall Street is named for a real wall. In the seventeenth century, Dutch colonists built a wall in lower Manhattan to help them defend against an expected British invasion.
> › Wall Street didn't become an official financial hub for another hundred years, when a group of local merchants signed an agreement under a famous buttonwood tree on Wall Street. The Buttonwood Agreement was the predecessor to the NYSE.

› Although U.S. stocks may lose money in a given year—or even over several years—they have always bounced back. Returns on the S&P 500 have never been negative over a twenty-year period.

Key Takeaways

› Stock exchanges link buyers with sellers and keep transactions flowing smoothly.

Economic growth	Higher economic growth = higher corporate profits = stocks go up
	Lower economic growth = lower corporate profits = stocks go down
Interest rates	Higher interest rates = stocks go down
	Lower interest rates = stocks go up
Tax rates	Taxes lowered on corporate profits = stocks go up
	Taxes raised on corporate profits = stocks go down
Inflation	Strong inflation or strong deflation = more uncertainty = stocks go down
	Moderate or steady inflation = less uncertainty = stocks go up
Economic growth in other countries	Higher economic growth = higher corporate sales to other countries = stocks go up
	Lower economic growth = lower corporate sales to other countries = stocks go down
Shocking events	Terrorist attacks, major weather events, or other big shocks = more uncertainty = stocks go down

> The stock market is made up of all individual stocks—so when individual stocks move, the market moves.
> Economic growth, interest rates, tax rates, and inflation can influence the broader stock market's movements.

Ninety percent of adulthood is getting excited about canceling plans and pretending to understand the stock market. —Napkin Finance ☺

Bull or Bear Market

Wall Street may be a bit of a rodeo, but there are no literal bulls or bears. Instead, these terms are trader lingo for describing how the stock market is performing.

Bull Market

A bull market is when stocks are generally rising. Bull markets tend to correspond with:

> A growing, or "expanding," economy.
> Falling or stable unemployment.
> Rising corporate profits.
> Stable or rising inflation.

Sometimes, you might also hear that an expert is "bullish" on the market, or "bullish" on some particular stock. That just means that person thinks the market, or a particular stock, is likely to go up.

BULL OR BEAR MARKET

WHAT

HOW THE STOCK MARKET IS DOING

BULL MARKET
STOCKS ARE RISING

- ECONOMY EXPANDING
- UNEMPLOYMENT FALLING OR STABLE
- AVG. LENGTH 9 YEARS

BEAR MARKET
STOCKS ARE FALLING

- ECONOMY CONTRACTING
- UNEMPLOYMENT RISING
- AVG. LENGTH 1 YEAR

OLD WALL STREET SAYING ABOUT GREED

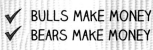

✓ BULLS MAKE MONEY
✓ BEARS MAKE MONEY

→ PIGS
GET SLAUGHTERED!

Bear Market

A bear market is a period when stocks are generally falling—or more specifically, a time when major stock indexes have fallen at least 20% (a fall of less than that would be called a "correction," but not a bear market). Bear markets tend to correspond with:

> › A shrinking, or "contracting," economy.
> › Rising unemployment.
> › Falling corporate profits.
> › Deflation, or unstable inflation.

And experts can also be "bearish" on a particular stock or asset class.

What It Means for You

Although those definitions make the stock market sound neat and orderly, in the real world it's a lot messier. If stocks fall for a few days in a row, it could be the start of a new bear market, or it could just be the market acting weird for a few days—after which it will keep marching up.

Investors waste a lot of energy (and money) trying to guess when a bull market is ending so that they can sell, or guess when a bear market is ending, so that they can buy. The reality is, no one can predict those turning points consistently. Most investors do a lot better by just holding on through bull and bear markets.

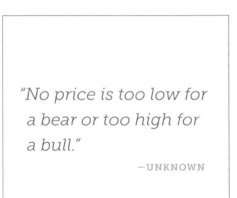

"No price is too low for a bear or too high for a bull."

—UNKNOWN

Fun Facts

› The average bull market has lasted 9.1 years, with the market returning an average of 480%.
› The average bear market has lasted 1.4 years, with average losses of 41%.
› The terms "bull" and "bear" are used for the way the animals attack: bulls thrust their horns up, while bears swipe their paws down.

Key Takeaways

› A bull market is a time when stocks are generally rising, and the economy is doing well.
› A bear market is a period when stocks are generally falling, and the economy is doing poorly.
› In a perfect world, you could predict when the market would turn so you could capture all the gains and suffer none of the losses. In the real world, the best bet is usually to hold on through ups and downs.

"The only ones to get hurt on a roller coaster are the jumpers."

—PAUL HARVEY, JOURNALIST

Your twenties are like a bull market for your metabolism while your fifties are like a bear market for your hair. —Napkin Finance ☺

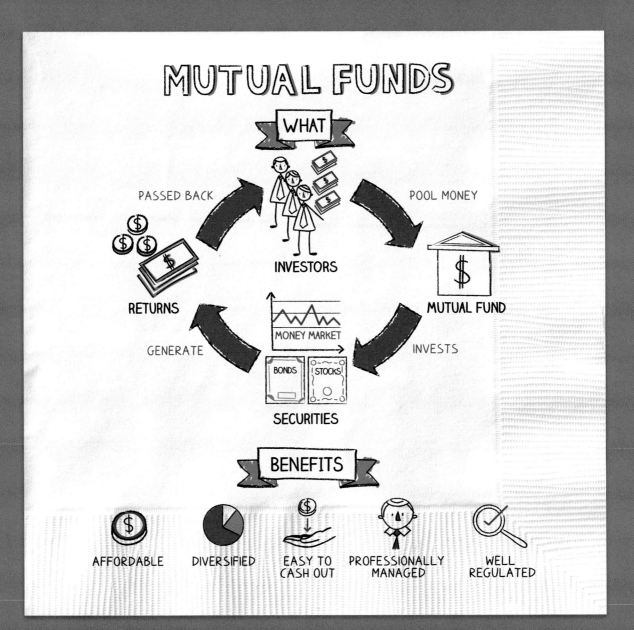

Mutual Funds

A mutual fund is a professionally managed fund that pools lots of investors' money in order to buy a basket of investments.

You can think of it this way: Picking your own stocks and bonds is a bit like cooking your own meals—you need to choose good ingredients, use some know-how in putting them together, and make sure that you're giving yourself a well-balanced diet. Investing in mutual funds is like hiring an affordable personal chef. Someone else is responsible for your meal planning and for all that legwork. But you still need to make sure you're being served a healthy diet (and not being overcharged).

How It Works

Step 1: Investors buy shares in the mutual fund.

Step 2: The fund pools investors' money and uses it to buy a portfolio of investments—typically stocks and bonds.

Step 3: Dividends, interest, and gains are paid back to investors, who can choose to reinvest them in the fund (you may choose what to do with this income when you initially invest in a fund, although you can typically update this option anytime).

Step 4: Investors can cash out of the mutual fund at any time.

Benefits

Mutual funds are a popular investment option because they offer:

› Professional management—By pooling money, funds can afford to hire top-notch managers. Some also have large teams of researchers and analysts.

> Diversification—Many funds own hundreds (or even thousands) of individual securities. Investors can build fully diversified portfolios with just one or two mutual funds.
> Liquidity—Although you can't trade them as frequently as stocks, you can usually buy or sell fund shares on any day the market's open.
> Affordability—Many funds let you invest with only a few hundred or thousand dollars to start. Mutual fund fees vary, but most are much cheaper than the typical hedge fund, and the cheapest funds cost only pennies for every $100 you invest.
> Oversight and regulation—Mutual funds must file periodic reports on their investments, report the value of what they own every day, and follow restrictions on what investments they can buy. It would be basically impossible for a mutual fund to pull off a Bernie Madoff–type fraud.

Types

There are mutual funds that invest in all kinds of things, including:

> Stock funds—invest in stocks.
> Bond funds—invest in bonds.
> Money-market funds—invest in very safe, short-term debt.
> Balanced funds—invest in a mix of stocks and bonds.
> Target-date funds—invest in a fully diversified mix of investments, which becomes more conservative as you near retirement.

Fun Facts

› A vigilant numbers geek named Harry Markopolos tried to warn U.S. regulators many times that Madoff was a fraud, including with a 2005 letter titled "The World's Largest Hedge Fund is a Fraud." The regulators didn't listen, and in 2008 Madoff's fund collapsed.

› The oldest mutual fund is the MFS Massachusetts Investors Trust fund, which launched in 1924.

Key Takeaways

› A mutual fund pools investors' money in order to buy a diversified portfolio of securities.

› The benefits of mutual funds include professional management, easy diversification, comparatively low fees, and strong regulatory oversight.

› Mutual funds can invest in a wide range of assets. How risky a particular fund is, or how much it returns, will depend on the underlying investments it holds.

Invest in a diversified mutual fund to lower the risk of your investments.
Invest in a gym membership to lower the risk of love handles.
—Napkin Finance ☺

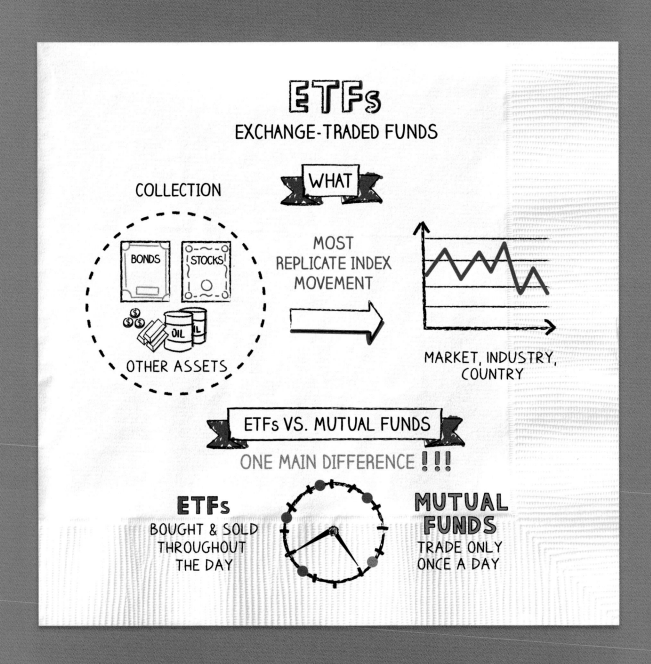

ETFs

Exchange-traded funds (ETFs), like stocks, trade on exchanges, but otherwise they're very similar to mutual funds. Like mutual funds, ETFs are professionally managed baskets of investments that investors can use to put together a broad, well-diversified portfolio.

ETFs vs. Mutual Funds

Here are the key differences:

ETFs	Mutual funds
Shares trade on exchanges just like stocks, meaning you can watch the price go up and down throughout the trading day.	Shares are valued once a day, not throughout the day.
Buy and sell shares throughout the trading day, just as you can with stocks.	Buy or redeem shares once a day.
Most are index funds—meaning they track an index's performance instead of trying to beat the market.	Some are index funds, but many are actively managed funds, meaning a manager tries to pick only the best investments.
Usually generate minimal tax bills as long as you hold on to your shares.	Can generate substantial tax bills even if you hold on to your shares.

Why Popular

ETFs have become incredibly popular in recent years for a few reasons:

- › Index investing is popular.
  - › There's good evidence to show that investors on average do better with index funds, which aim only to match the market's returns, than they do with actively managed funds, which aim to beat the market's returns.
- › Fees can be even lower than with mutual funds.
  - › Although you can buy index mutual funds, index ETFs can have even lower fees (and higher fees = lower returns).
- › Low initial investment.
  - › You can start investing for the price of just one share. (Mutual funds can require minimum initial investments in the thousands of dollars.)
- › You can invest in almost anything with them.
  - › Just as with mutual funds, ETFs can hold traditional stocks and bonds. But you can also use them to invest in things that are farther afield. For example, there are ETFs that hold physical gold, that track the day-to-day movements of oil prices, and that invest exclusively in biotech stocks.

Fun Facts

› The SPDR Gold Shares ETF holds about seventy thousand bars of gold (each weighing four hundred ounces) in an HSBC vault in London. Once a year it hires a firm to count every single bar in the vault to make sure they're all there (hello, summer internship).

› There is almost $4 trillion invested in ETFs in the U.S.

› The world of ETFs can get pretty weird. See: the Obesity ETF, the Global X Millennials Thematic ETF, and the HealthShares Dermatology and Wound Care ETF.

Key Takeaways

› ETFs are similar to mutual funds, but unlike mutual funds they trade throughout the day on stock exchanges.

› Most ETFs are index funds, meaning they track the performance of an index, such as the S&P 500.

› ETFs have become wildly popular in recent years as investors have moved money into index funds, and thanks to their lower cost and tax advantage over mutual funds.

You can't spell "exchange-traded funds" without *fun*!*
*Definitions of fun may vary. —Napkin Finance ☺

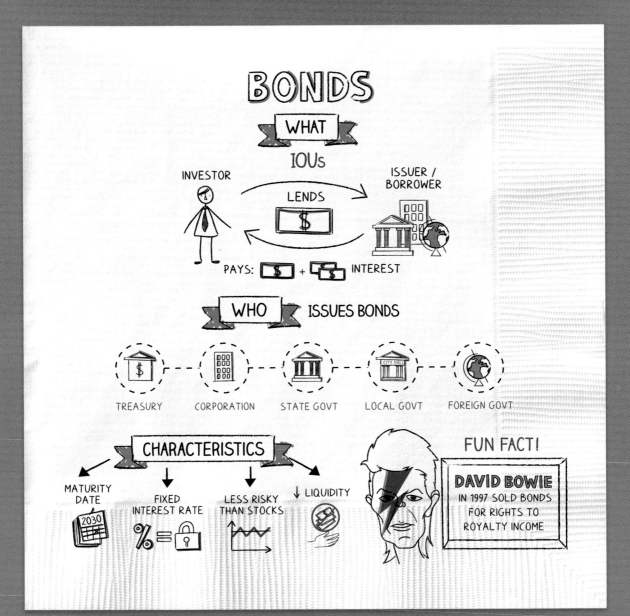

Bonds

Bonds are essentially IOUs. When you buy a bond, you become a lender to whatever entity issued the bond. Typically, the borrower pays you a certain amount of interest periodically. When the bond matures, it also pays you back your initial investment, or the principal value of the bond.

Features

Bonds have some main characteristics that distinguish them from stocks:

›   Fixed interest rate—Most bonds pay a set rate that never changes. If a bond has a face value of $1,000 and a 5% interest rate, it pays $50 per year.

›   Maturity date—Some bonds mature after thirty years and some after one year. But most bonds have a specific end date on which they repay your initial investment.

›   Credit rating—A credit rating assesses how likely a particular bond issuer is to make its interest and principal payments.
    ›   Top-notch bonds are rated "AAA."
    ›   Low-rated bonds are called junk bonds. They pay higher interest rates, but because they're issued by financially shaky companies they're more likely to default.

›   Lower risk and lower returns—Bonds generally return less and are less risky than stocks.

›   Harder to buy and sell—Stocks are easy to trade with any major broker. But it can be hard to buy individual bonds on your own, and you often don't get a great price if you need to sell them.

Types

The main categories of bonds are:

> › Treasuries—Issued by the federal government. You get a tax break on your state and local taxes on your interest income from Treasuries.
> › Municipals—Issued by state and local governments and related entities. You typically get a tax break on your federal taxes on interest income, and sometimes on state and local taxes as well.
> › Corporates—Issued by corporations. There are no tax breaks on interest income.

Fun Facts

> › In 1997 David Bowie sold bonds that gave bondholders the rights to his royalty income. The Bowie bonds paid 8%.
> › Disney, Coca-Cola, and the countries of Argentina and Austria have all issued one-hundred-year bonds.

Key Takeaways

> › Bonds are debts. When you buy a bond, you become a lender and the issuer becomes a borrower.
> › Bonds generally pay a set interest rate and mature on a particular date.
> › They're generally less risky than stocks and return less than stocks.

The difference between Peter Pan and a bond is that eventually a bond will mature and pay you a bunch of money. —Napkin Finance ☺

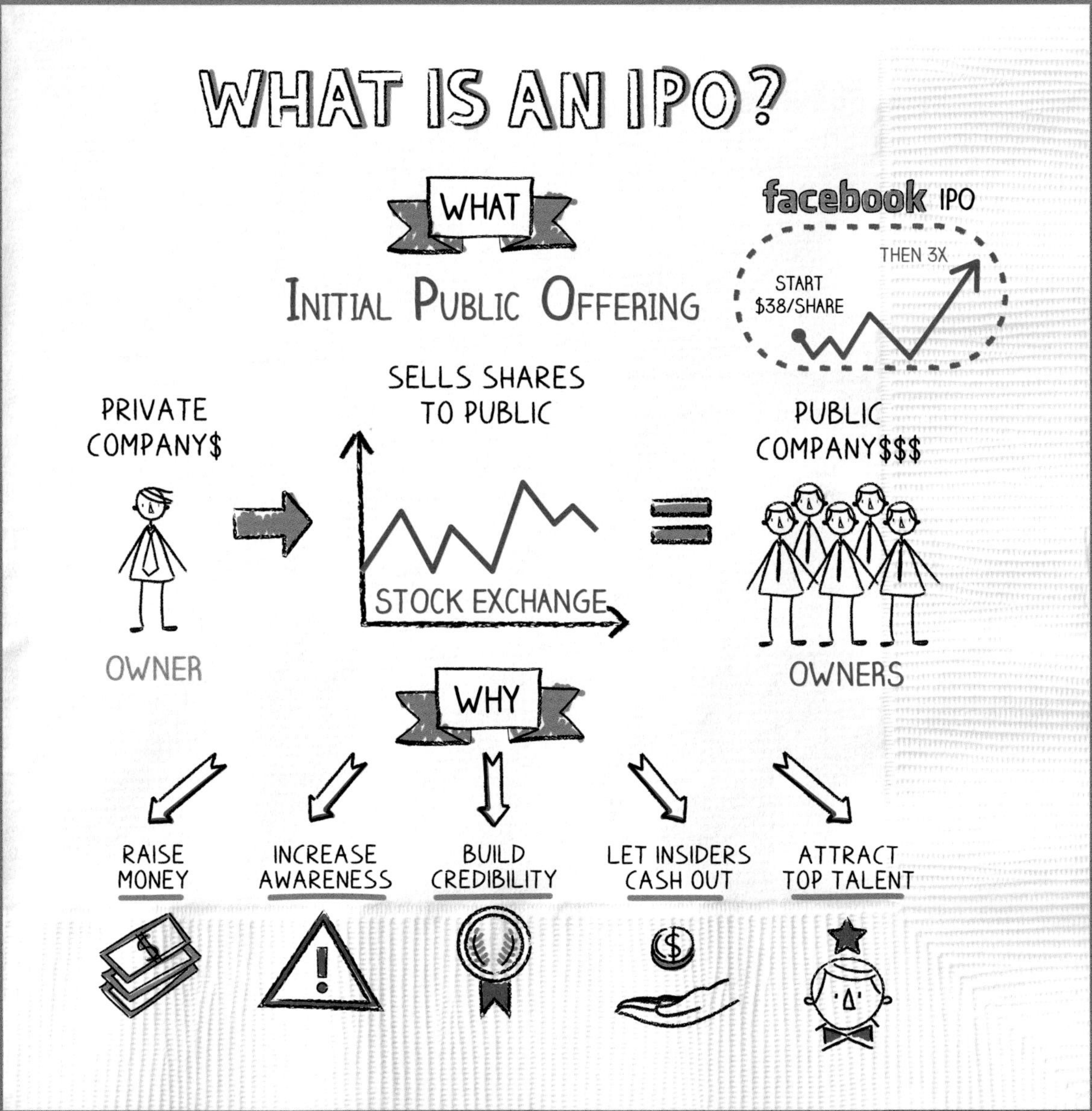
WHAT IS AN IPO?
WHAT
INITIAL PUBLIC OFFERING
facebook IPO
START $38/SHARE
THEN 3X
SELLS SHARES TO PUBLIC
PRIVATE COMPANY$
STOCK EXCHANGE
PUBLIC COMPANY$$$
OWNER
OWNERS
WHY
RAISE MONEY
INCREASE AWARENESS
BUILD CREDIBILITY
LET INSIDERS CASH OUT
ATTRACT TOP TALENT

What Is an IPO?

An initial public offering, or IPO, is when a company's shares start trading on a stock exchange and when average people can start investing in the company. It's also called "going public."

How It Works

Step 1: A company starts out as a private company, meaning it doesn't have shares that trade. Insiders such as the founders or employees typically own most of the company.

Step 2: The company decides to go public. It hires an investment bank to help it figure out the details—such as how many shares to sell and at what price.

Step 3: The company files an S-1 statement with regulators. This form is like a heads-up that the company plans to go public, and it includes details on how much money will be raised, plus information about the company's finances.

Step 4: The investment bank buys up the chunk of shares that's going to be offered.

Step 5: IPO day: The shares start trading on whatever exchange they are listed on, and the investment bank sells its shares to the public.

Why IPO?

The main reason companies go public is to raise money, which they need to expand their businesses. Some additional reasons may include to:

> › Let insiders cash out—Early employees could hold valuable ownership positions in the company, but have no way of selling their stakes. After an IPO, they can finally sell their shares (and take that cash straight to the Tesla dealership).
> › Get bragging rights—Companies may want the credibility and prestige of having their shares traded on a major exchange.
> › Raise awareness—Having a big, splashy IPO can get potential investors excited about the company.
> › Attract talent—With publicly traded shares, it can be easier to offer stock compensation plans to employees, which can make the company a more attractive place to work.

IPOs vs. Secondary Offerings

A company can sell more shares in the future even after having an IPO. Those sales are called "secondary offerings," and they usually happen with less of a bang than IPOs.

Fun Facts

> › When a company IPOs on the New York Stock Exchange, its executives get to ring the bell on the trading floor to start the day's trading.
> › Great IPOs can make terrible stocks and vice versa. Snapchat stock gained 44% on its first day of trading, then lost more than 75% of its value in the next few years. Facebook shares fell when they first started trading, but gained about 300% in the following years.
> › It's possible for a company to go public without an IPO. Spotify did so with a so-called "direct listing" in 2018. The downside is a direct listing doesn't allow the company to raise *new* money (it only lets existing

investors cash out). The upside is that because direct listings are less hyped than IPOs, they tend to be less volatile than IPO stocks.

Key Takeaways

› An IPO is when a company's shares start trading in the stock market. It can also be called "going public."
› Companies go public to raise funds but may also use it as a chance to raise awareness or let existing investors cash out.

If you bought shares of Google at its IPO you could probably hire a butler to Google things for you now. —Napkin Finance ☺

Chapter Quiz

1. **Stocks are:**

   a. Forms of debt.
   b. Expensive wall decor.
   c. Pieces of ownership in companies.
   d. Socks made out of steel. *Stocks!*

2. **The two ways investors earn returns on stocks are:**

   a. Dividends and price gains.
   b. Interest and principal.
   c. Fear and intimidation.
   d. IOUs and Bed Bath & Beyond coupons.

3. **True or false: The words** *stocks, shares,* **and** *equities* **all mean the same thing.**

   ○ True   ○ False

4. **To trade stocks, you typically need to:**

   a. Know the secret handshake.
   b. Go to the physical stock exchange.
   c. First check some Reddit forums for hot and very accurate stock tips.
   d. Set up an account with a broker.

5. **Things that tend to make the stock market go up include:**

   a. A stronger U.S. dollar and higher tariffs.
   b. Lower interest rates and lower taxes.
   c. Elon Musk having a good hair day.
   d. Viagra.

6. **True or false: U.S. stocks have never lost money over a twenty-year period.**

   ○ True   ○ False

7. **A bull market is when:**

   a. Investors get gored.
   b. Stocks rise.
   c. Bonds fall.
   d. Your grocery store has a sale on red meat.

8. **If your Uber driver says he's "bearish" on tech stocks, it means he:**

   a. Thinks tech stocks will fall in price.
   b. Thinks tech stocks will rise in price.
   c. Has no idea how to get to your destination.
   d. Deserves a one-star rating.

9. **A mutual fund is:**

   a. A type of crowdsourced investment.
   b. A fund that you can only invest in if it likes you back.
   c. An exchange-traded fund.
   d. An investment that pools investors' money and is run by a professional manager.

10. **The benefits of mutual funds include all of the following, except:**

    a. Strong regulation.
    b. Professional management.
    c. Guaranteed performance.
    d. Diversification.

11. **ETFs are:**

    a. Funds that only elves can invest in.
    b. Funds that are managed by fortune-tellers.
    c. Funds that trade on exchanges, like stocks.
    d. Easy To Forgive.

12. **ETFs are popular for all of the following reasons except:**

    a. They tend to have low fees.
    b. Investors can get started with a small initial investment.
    c. Index investing is popular, and most ETFs are index funds.
    d. They have a longer track record than mutual funds.

13. **Compared with stocks, bonds typically:**

    a. Are lower risk and lower return.
    b. Pay higher dividends.
    c. Are easier to buy and sell.
    d. Are shaken, not stirred.

14. **Credit ratings for bonds range from:**
    a. AAA to ZZZ.
    b. AAA to junk.
    c. Meh to Awww Yea!
    d. Blue Steel to Magnum.

15. **True or false: Investors get a tax break on interest income from corporate bonds.**

    ○ True   ○ False

16. **IPO stands for:**
    a. Illegal Pet Owners.
    b. Investment Primary Opening.
    c. Initial Public Offering.
    d. I'm Purchasing Oreos.

17. **A company's reasons for going public may include all of the following except:**
    a. Raising money.
    b. Letting insiders cash out their shares.
    c. Attracting top employees.
    d. Saving money on accountants and lawyers.

Answers

1. c	**6.** t	**11.** c	**16.** c
2. a	**7.** b	**12.** d	**17.** d
3. t	**8.** a	**13.** a	
4. d	**9.** d	**14.** b	
5. b	**10.** c	**15.** f	

7

EZ Does It

TAXES

TAXES

WHAT

FUNDS THAT **PEOPLE** & **COMPANIES** PAY TO THE **GOVERNMENT**

CORPORATION

CONTRIBUTION

$

TYPES OF TAXES

PERSONAL INCOME   SALES   CAPITAL GAINS   ESTATE   PROPERTY   CORPORATE INCOME

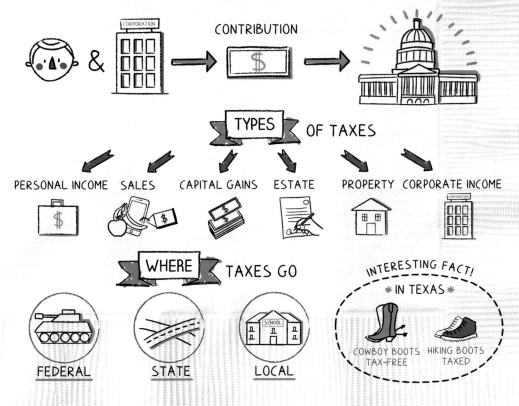

WHERE TAXES GO

FEDERAL   STATE   LOCAL

SCHOOL

INTERESTING FACT!
* IN TEXAS *

COWBOY BOOTS
TAX-FREE

HIKING BOOTS
TAXED

Taxes

Taxes are funds that people and companies must pay to the government.

Types

The government wants a piece of the action pretty much any time a person or company earns money. Here are a few ways we all pay:

> › Income tax—You pay this on your salary, but also on most gig-economy income and investment income.
> › Sales tax—You pay when you buy something in a store, or a restaurant, or online.
> › Property tax—You pay if you own real estate.
> › Capital gains tax—You may owe if you sell an investment for a profit.
> › Estate tax—When someone wealthy dies, the government will probably get a cut.
> › Corporate income tax—The government gets a slice of corporate profits.

Where Your Taxes Go

Your taxes pay for all kinds of things, from senators' paychecks to fixing bridges to funding foreign aid. More specifically:

> › Federal income tax goes to the U.S. federal government, and pays for:
>   › Military spending.
>   › Social Security.
>   › Medicare and Medicaid.
>   › Interest payments on the national debt, and more.

- State sales and income taxes pay for:
  - Public schools.
  - Medicaid.
  - Transportation.
  - State prisons, and more.
- Property taxes and other local taxes pay for:
  - Public schools.
  - Fire and police departments.
  - Road maintenance, and more.

> *"Taxes are what we pay for a civilized society."*
>
> —OLIVER WENDELL HOLMES, JR., SUPREME COURT JUSTICE

Fun Facts

- In Texas, cowboy boots are exempt from sales tax but hiking boots are not.
- If you buy a whole bagel in New York, you don't pay a sales tax. If the store slices the bagel for you then it's considered prepared food, and you do pay sales tax.
- In Kansas, riding a hot air balloon that's tethered to the ground is subject to an amusement tax. If it's not tethered then it is considered a form of transportation and your ride is tax-free.
- New Mexico residents who live to one hundred get a break for the rest of their lives on state income tax.

Key Takeaways

- Taxes are what people and companies pay so that the government can function.

> You may pay taxes on what you earn, what you buy, and property you own.
> You may pay taxes at the federal, state, and local levels—which go to pay for different types of services.

Teach your kids about taxes by eating 38% of their french fries.
—Napkin Finance ☹

Tax Returns

Most people pay taxes throughout the year. When you file a tax return, you calculate how much you legally owed for the year and compare it to how much you paid. If you paid too little then you send a check in for the rest with your return. If you paid too much then you sit back and wait for your refund.

Filing your tax returns is important because you do not want to mess with the IRS. Ever.

How It Works

Step 1: During the calendar year, you probably pay taxes through payroll. If you have other income, you may pay quarterly estimated taxes as well.

> *"The only two things that scare me are God and the IRS."*
>
> —DR. DRE, RAPPER AND PRODUCER

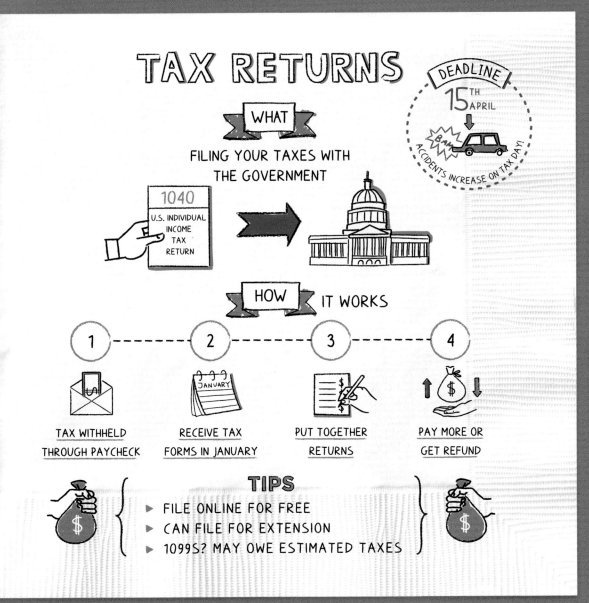

Step 2: In late January, your employer (or employers) and any financial institutions you have accounts with should send you your tax forms.

Step 3: By April 15 (but after you've exhausted every option for procrastination), you put together your return.

Step 4: If you owe money, you generally send in a payment with your return. If you're due a refund, you'll probably receive it in the weeks after you file.

What You Need

To put together your return, you'll at least need:

> › Your Social Security number.
> › Last year's return.
> › Any W-2s or 1099s from employers.
> › Any 1099s from financial institutions.
> › Records for any deductions or credits you'll be taking.

(And a bottle of wine, to help you forget the trauma of filing your taxes.)

Good to Know

> › You can file your taxes online with the IRS for free. Some tax-software companies also offer free returns if your taxes are very simple or if you make less than a certain amount.
> › If you can't make the deadline, you can file for an extension to get another six months to put together your return. (An extension only gives you more time for the form. If you owe money, the IRS would still like that now, please.)

> If you're in the gig economy, chances are you need to be filing and paying estimated taxes four times a year.

Fun Facts

> Other countries have it better. Germany, Japan, and Spain are among the thirty-six countries in which citizens don't have to file a tax return (the government does all the number crunching).
> The rate of fatal car crashes tends to go up on April 15. All the more reason to e-file.

Key Takeaways

> Your annual tax return is where you add up how much you owe the government for the last year and how much you already paid, and reconcile the difference.
> You'll need any W-2s, 1099s, other records of income, and records for deductions and credits in order to file your tax return.

Remember, your tax returns are more afraid of you than you are of them.
—Napkin Finance ☺

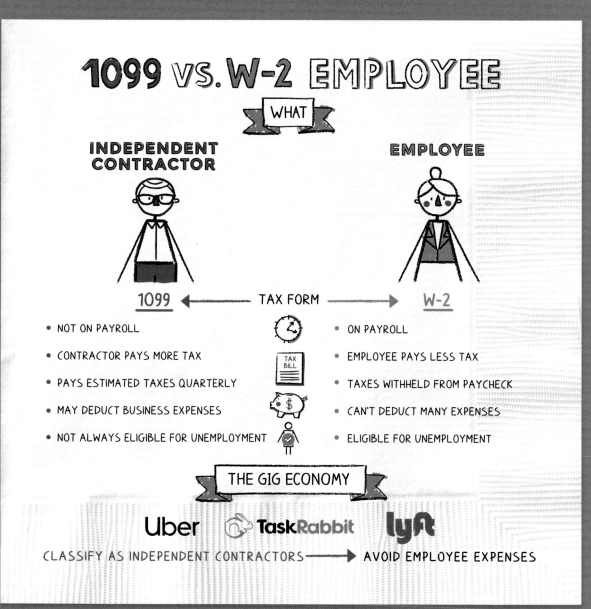

1099 vs. W-2 Employee

1099s and W-2s are both types of tax forms. If you're a contractor, you should receive one or more 1099s at the end of the year. If you're an employee, you should receive a W-2.

Why Important

Whether you are classified as a contractor or employee affects both how much you pay in taxes and when you pay. It can also affect what benefits you're eligible for:

	Contractor	Employee
Tax form	1099	W-2
When you pay taxes	Pay estimated taxes four times a year.	Taxes withheld from your paychecks.
You pay	More tax	Less tax
Your employer pays	Less tax	More tax
Benefits?	May not be eligible for unemployment if you lose your job. Not eligible for health insurance, 401(k), or other company benefits.	Generally eligible for unemployment if you lose your job. Usually eligible for health insurance, 401(k), or other company benefits.

How Decided

You can tell whether you're treated as a contractor or an employee by what type of tax form you receive and how you're paid. If you're paid every two weeks through payroll and you receive a W-2 at the end of the year, you're an employee. If you submit invoices for your work and you receive a 1099 at the end of the year, you're a contractor.

The factors that decide this distinction include:

› How much control you have over the work you do.
  › You have more control → contractor
  › You have less control → employee
› Whether you pay for your work-related expenses, or your employer does.
  › You pay for your expenses → contractor
  › The company pays → employee
› Whether or not you're free to seek out additional work in the same field on the side.
  › You can have side gigs → contractor
  › You can't → employee
› How integral your contribution is to the business.
  › Less integral → contractor
  › More integral → employee
› Whether your gig is essentially permanent, or will only last for a specific project or period.
  › Specific period → contractor
  › Essentially permanent → employee

Good to Know

It's not always straightforward how someone should be classified, and the decision can be controversial.

Gig-economy companies, such as Uber, Lyft, and TaskRabbit, generally classify their workers as contractors (because it's cheaper for them). But there's been ongoing legal drama over whether they should really be treated as employees.

Fun Facts

› If you're an employee and you hit someone while driving your car for work, then your employer is probably liable. If you're a contractor and you hit someone while driving your car for work, then you're probably liable.

› Even the government can't always make up its mind on how people should be classified. Different federal government agencies (such as the IRS and the Department of Labor) can have different opinions, as can different states or courts. You could have one status for your taxes but another status for another purpose (such as if you're resolving a labor dispute or if you're sued for that car accident).

Key Takeaways

› Whether you receive a 1099 or W-2 tax form depends on whether you are a contractor or employee.

› Your classification affects how much you pay in taxes, when you pay, and what benefits you're eligible for.

› How you should be classified can be complicated and depends on several factors.

Beyoncé is an independent contractor, so if you receive a 1099 you have something in common with Beyoncé! —Napkin Finance ☺

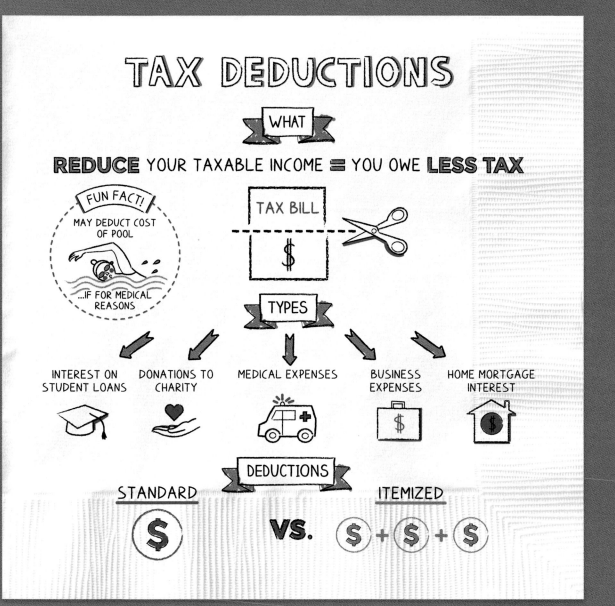

Tax Deductions

Tax deductions, such as for donations to charity or interest on student loans, are amounts that you subtract from your income when calculating how much you owe in taxes. Claiming tax deductions helps you pay less tax.

If you earned $50,000 for the year but took $10,000 in deductions, the amount of tax you pay would be based on $40,000 of income.

Common Types

Some of the main deductions include:

> *"Few of us ever test our powers of deduction, except when filling out an income tax form."*
>
> —LAURENCE J. PETER, AUTHOR

- › Interest on student loans.
- › IRA contributions.
- › State and local taxes.
- › Interest on your home mortgage.
- › Donations to charity.
- › Medical expenses, if your expenses for the year reached a certain percentage of your income.
- › Business expenses, if you run your own business.

Deductions vs. Credits

Both credits and deductions reduce what you owe in taxes. But tax credits give you more bang for your buck because they reduce your taxes dollar for dollar (while deductions reduce the amount of income you owe tax on).

Suppose you earned $50,000 and your tax rate is 25% (real-life rates are more complicated than this). Here's how a deduction of $10,000 would work out, compared with a credit of $10,000:

	$10,000 deduction	$10,000 credit
Your taxable income is:	$50,000 - $10,000 = $40,000	$50,000
At 25%, your taxes are:	$40,000 x 0.25 = $10,000	$50,000 x 0.25 = $12,500
Minus credits:	-$0	-$10,000
Total tax you pay:	$10,000	$2,500

Itemized vs. Standard

Everyone must choose between taking the standard deduction or itemizing. The standard deduction is simpler—there's a set dollar amount that you deduct from your income, and you don't need to do a lot of math or record keeping. Itemizing is more complicated but results in bigger savings for some people—you figure out all the specific deductions you're eligible for and add them up.

Some specific deductions you can still take even if you don't itemize (such as the student-loan interest deduction). But many you can't take unless you itemize (such as the deductions for mortgage interest and charity donations).

Fun Facts

› Work expenses are often tax-deductible, and the definition of *work expense* may be broader than you think. A stripper was reportedly able to deduct the cost of breast augmentation surgery, after a judge ruled her implants were stage props.
› You may be able to deduct the cost of a swimming pool or home renovations if you need the pool or the renovations for medical reasons.

"There may be liberty and justice for all, but there are tax breaks only for some."

—MARTIN A. SULLIVAN, ECONOMIST

Key Takeaways

› Tax deductions reduce what you pay in taxes by lowering the amount of income your taxes are calculated on.
› Common tax deductions include breaks for student-loan interest, mortgage interest, and some retirement-plan contributions.
› Tax deductions are great, but credits can be even better because they reduce the tax you owe dollar for dollar.

Home is where your tax refund is sent. —Napkin Finance ☺

Chapter Quiz

1. **Types of tax include all of the following, except:**

    a. Income tax.

    b. Capital gains tax.

    c. Turbo tax.

    d. Property tax.

2. **Taxes pay for:**

    a. The sun to come out.

    b. The Internet.

    c. Botox.

    d. Public schools and the military.

3. **True or false: Property taxes go to fund the federal government.**

    ○ True   ○ False

4. **Your tax return is:**

    a. When the government returns the taxes you've paid to you.

    b. When you reconcile how much tax you've already paid for a given year with what you actually owe for that year.

    c. What you use to fund a Vegas trip.

    d. A good opportunity to engage in political protest by not paying your taxes.

5. **Filing your taxes after the mid-April deadline is:**

    a. Fine as long as you've filed for an extension.

    b. Fine as long as you live off the grid.

    c. Punishable by death.

    d. The new skydiving.

6. **True or false: You can file your taxes online for free.**

   ○ True   ○ False

7. **To file your taxes you need all of the following except:**
   a. Last year's tax return.
   b. Your Social Security number.
   c. All of your bank statements for the past year.
   d. Any 1099s or W-2s you've received.

8. **If you're a contractor, it means:**
   a. The government doesn't know how much money you make so you don't have to pay taxes on it.
   b. You'll generally pay estimated taxes four times a year and receive 1099s in January.
   c. The companies you work for pay taxes on your behalf.
   d. You write screenplays at Starbucks.

9. **Perks of being treated as an employee include:**
   a. You pay less tax on your earnings and you're generally eligible for unemployment benefits if you lose your job.
   b. Your employer files your taxes on your behalf.
   c. Free office supplies.
   d. Bottling up your rage until you implode.

10. **Factors that affect whether you should be classified as an employee or a contractor include:**
    a. How many hours a day you're on Facebook.
    b. How much lying goes into calling in sick.
    c. Whether you receive tips at work.
    d. How much control you have over the work you do and who pays for your work expenses.

11. **Tax deductions are:**
    a. A legal way of paying less tax.
    b. Only relevant for the super-rich.
    c. Something you don't need to worry about because your parents handle those for you, right?
    d. How you convinced yourself to buy a ninety-inch TV.

12. **True or false: Tax deductions reduce how much tax you owe dollar for dollar.**
    ○ True   ○ False

13. **Tax deductions include all of the following except:**
    a. Charitable donations.
    b. Pet expenses.
    c. Interest on student loans.
    d. Business expenses.

14. **The main choice to make when figuring out your deductions is:**
    a. Which parent you should call to ask how this all works.
    b. Whether you should take a full or a partial deduction.
    c. How many children you should say you have.
    d. Whether to itemize or take the standard deduction.

15. **True or false: In some cases, it's possible to deduct the cost of home renovations.**
    ○ True   ○ False

Answers

1. c	**5.** a	**9.** a	**13.** b
2. d	**6.** t	**10.** d	**14.** d
3. f	**7.** c	**11.** a	**15.** t
4. b	**8.** b	**12.** f	

8

Go Big

STARTING A COMPANY

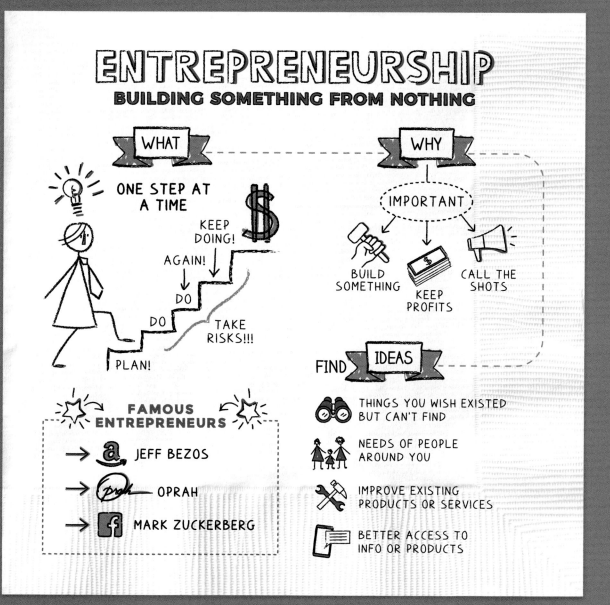

Entrepreneurship

Entrepreneurship is the spirit of innovation. It means coming up with an idea and taking the initiative to make that idea a reality.

Although the word *entrepreneur* may bring to mind business moguls such as Jeff Bezos, Oprah, or Mark Zuckerberg, anyone who's running their own business or side gig counts as an entrepreneur.

> *"If you don't build your dream, someone will hire you to help build theirs."*
>
> —TONY A. GASKINS, JR., AUTHOR

Pros and Cons

To be the boss, you have to pay the cost:

Pros	Cons
You keep your profits.	You take all the risk.
Chance to build something you love and leave a legacy.	Even great ideas can fail.
You call the shots and hire your team.	More responsibility = more stress.

Myths About Entrepreneurship

Chasing your dreams can be scary, but don't let these misconceptions hold you back.

Myth	Fact
You need already to be rich to start a business.	Some businesses can get off the ground with little initial money, but many raise funds from outside investors or lenders to get started.
You need a completely original, unique, and brilliant idea.	Plenty of successful businesses are based on existing products and services.
Failure is your enemy.	Many successful entrepreneurs have a string of failures before they get a hit. Learn from your mistakes, but don't be afraid of making them.

How to Come Up with Ideas

You don't necessarily need a blindingly original idea, but you do need an idea. Try keeping a journal, and make a note any time you think of:

> › Products or services that you wish existed but can't find.
> › Needs of those around you that aren't being met by existing products.
> › Ways existing products or services could be better.
> › Ways to help people access information or products more easily.

Fun Facts

> › If you want a good luck charm for your new business, start it in a garage. Companies that reportedly started in garages include Apple, Amazon, Google, and Disney.
> › The world record for inventions is held by Shunpei Yamazaki, who holds more than eleven thousand patents.

Key Takeaways

› Entrepreneurship is the process of bringing your business idea into the world.
› When you're an entrepreneur, you can have the chance of a large payoff in profits and satisfaction, but you also take on your business's financial and reputational risk.
› To come up with ideas, keep a list in a journal of products or services that don't yet exist or that could be better.

Some successful entrepreneurs include Oprah, Jeff Bezos, and the clever Girl Scouts selling cookies outside weed dispensaries. —Napkin Finance ☺

How to Start a Start-Up

Although plenty of start-ups fail, the ones that succeed can do so wildly. Beyond a financial payoff, creating a start-up can give you the chance to create something meaningful, to disrupt the status quo—and yes, even to change the world.

The Basics

All start-ups are different, but most need each of these four things:

› Idea—maybe your start-up will disrupt an industry, make a product or service better, or meet a need that people didn't even know they had.
› Team—find a group of people you can work with whose skill sets complement yours. Start with three main roles: business, technical, and creative.

HOW TO START A START-UP

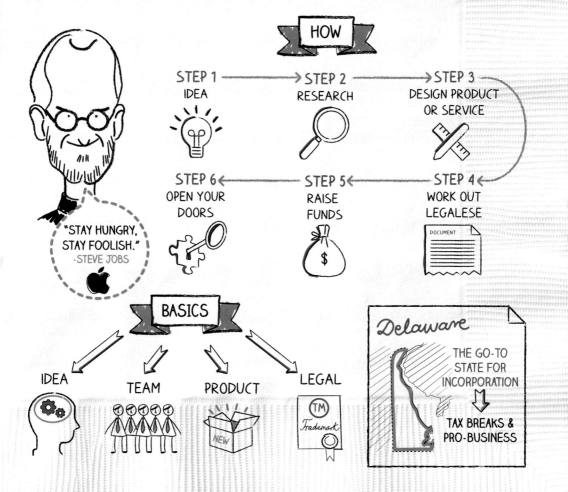

> › Product—develop a prototype of your product, a model for your service, or at least a realistic plan for how you'll develop your first products.
> › Legal—figure out your business structure, your name, and other legal issues.

Process

Step 1: Come up with your idea.

Step 2: Research the market. Who would your competitors be? Who would your customers be? How strong might demand for your product or service be?

Step 3: Make a plan. Design your product or service.

Step 4: Figure out the legalese. Decide on a business structure. Pick a name and file for any licenses or permits.

Step 5: Raise funds. Do you want to sell ownership stakes or take on a loan?

Step 6: Get the word out. Create some excitement for your new business.

Step 7: Open your doors.

Types

Although you may need a fresh idea, there are only a certain number of business models under the sun. Consider whether your company should:

> › Sell ads—start a free website or app that draws people in, and pay for it with ads.
> › Create a marketplace—think Etsy or eBay.
> › Sell goods or services to consumers—you could invent the next fidget spinner.

> Sell goods or services to businesses—solve a need for a specific industry.
> Go peer to peer—think Airbnb or ride shares.
> Sell intellectual property—develop something that you can license for a fee.

Fun Facts

> There are more "unicorn" companies—meaning start-ups worth $1 billion or more—based in California than anywhere else in the world.
> Many companies choose to incorporate in Delaware (even if they're headquartered elsewhere), because the state has a well-developed corporate law system and charges no income tax on companies that don't do business there.

Key Takeaways

> Launching a start-up can give you a chance at making it big.
> To start a new company, you first need an idea, a team, a product, and some help with legalese.
> Although it may seem difficult to come up with an idea, you can get inspiration from existing business models.

When you're starting a start-up you'll sleep like a baby: You'll wake up every two hours and cry a lot. —Napkin Finance ☺

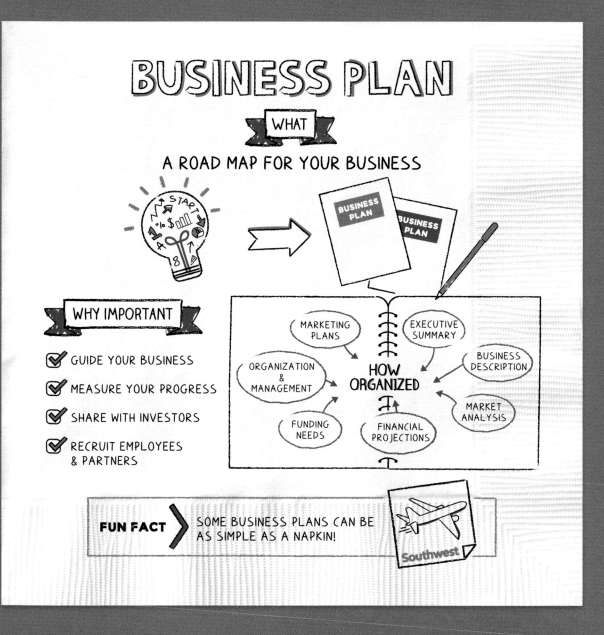

Business Plan

A business plan is a document that outlines your vision for your business. It describes your big-picture dream for where your company is going, but also includes some of the nuts-and-bolts steps you'll need to take to make your dream a reality.

Why Important

You'll use your business plan to:

> › Stay on track—Your plan can help you set out the exact steps you'll need to take to develop your business, so you always know what comes next.
> › Measure your progress—Put some milestones in your business plan that you can check off as your company grows.
> › Court investors—Prospective backers will want to know that you have a realistic plan, and may have questions about nitty-gritty details, such as any financial projections.
> › Recruit employees and partners— Having a realistic vision can help persuade top-notch employees, customers, and partners to work with you.

"We have a strategic plan. It's called 'doing things.'"

—HERB KELLEHER, COFOUNDER OF SOUTHWEST AIRLINES

How to Create

Your business plan can be as simple or as detailed as you choose to make it. Some business plans are drawn up on the back of a napkin. Others can be as long as a book.

You can consider including the following in your business plan:

> *It takes as much energy to wish as it does to plan.*
> —ELEANOR ROOSEVELT, ACTIVIST AND FORMER FIRST LADY

> › Executive summary—A quick overview of your whole plan.
> › Business description—The basics of your business model and what your company has accomplished so far.
> › Market analysis—Who are your customers and who are your competitors?
> › Organization and management—What's your company's legal structure? Who are the superstars on your team?
> › Marketing plans—Your plan for getting the word out about your business and finding customers.
> › Funding needs—How much money do you need to get off the ground?
> › Financial projections—Your best estimate of your company's sales and profits for its first few years.

Fun Facts

> › Southwest Airlines, *Shark Week,* trickle-down economics, and no fewer than four Pixar movies were all supposedly conceived of on napkins.

› In real-world Silicon Valley, founders are known to exaggerate facts and figures about their businesses when they pitch their plans to prospective investors. As one founder said, "Being honest in Silicon Valley is like being the one member of an Olympic team that isn't on steroids."

Key Takeaways

› Your business plan is your company's road map.
› You need a business plan for yourself and for potential investors, employees, and business partners.
› Some business plans will be extremely detailed while others may be more of a simple vision statement.

A business plan is a road map for your company and a prenup is a road map for your future divorce. —Napkin Finance ☺

Financing a Start-Up

Unless you're starting a business that doesn't need much cash to get going, you're going to need funding to get your company off the ground. The type of financing you'll need may depend on what stage of development your business is in, how much money you need, and whether you're comfortable giving up some ownership in your company.

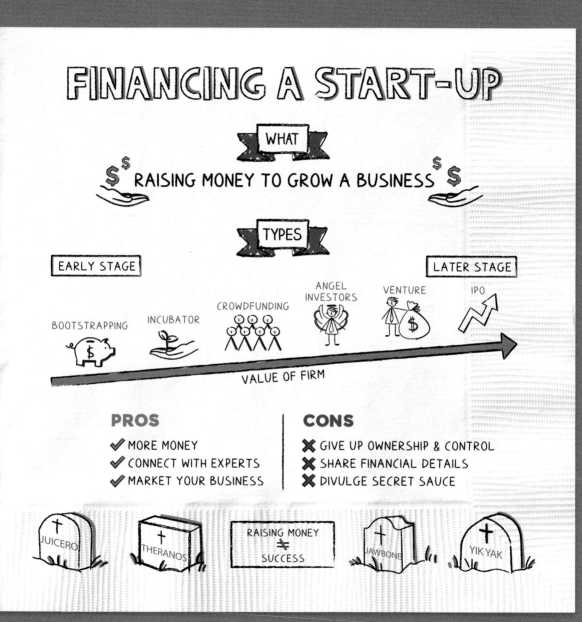

Types

Funding source	Stage	How it works
Bootstrapping	Very early	Tap personal sources of funds, such as savings, investments, home equity, or even a credit card.
Friends and family	Very early	Ask those who believe in your idea for a loan to get off the ground.
Incubator program	Very early	Get accepted into a development program for young companies, where you'll have resources to help you work out your idea and access to mentors.
Crowdfunding	Early	Put a description of your business plan online on a crowdfunding website and let the money come to you. (For more on this option, see chapter 12.)
Traditional lenders	Early	Apply for a small-business loan with your bank or credit union.
Angel investor	Early	Find a wealthy individual who's willing to write a big check in exchange for an ownership stake.
Accelerator program	Medium	Once your idea has some traction, apply and get accepted into a short-term start-up boot camp to fuel your growth.
Venture capital	Medium	Sell an ownership stake to sophisticated start-up investors.
IPO	Late	List your company's shares on a stock exchange and get access to funding from a large number of investors.
Issuing bonds	Late	Once your company is established, sell bonds that mature in 10, 20, or 30 years and pay a set interest rate.

Pros and Cons of Outside Funding

Taking on outside funding can be important to continuing growth, but it comes with trade-offs.

Pros	Cons
Get access to vastly more money.	Give up some ownership; give up some control.
Connect with mentors and experts.	Share your company's financials.
Market your business model.	Divulge your business model's secret sauce.

Fun Facts

> It can pay to keep control. Native Deodorant, a natural deodorant start-up, was sold for $100 million to Procter & Gamble just two and a half years after it launched. Its founder still owned more than 90% of the company.

> Juicero was a start-up that sold $400 machines that would squeeze a juice pack into a cup—like a Keurig for fruits and veggies. The company raised $120 million before anyone noticed that you could just squeeze its juice packs by hand—no fancy machine necessary. (The company shut down.)

Key Takeaways

> Most start-ups need money to get up and running.

> There are a wide array of funding sources, from self-funding to seeking out professional investors to borrowing from a bank.

> › Bringing in outside investors means gaining access to resources and expertise in exchange for giving up control and ownership.

Financing a start-up can be difficult, but not as difficult as parallel parking.
—Napkin Finance ☺

Chapter Quiz

1. **Entrepreneurship can mean:**
   a. Creating an app.
   b. Opening a restaurant.
   c. Selling crafts online.
   d. All of the above.

2. **The benefits of entrepreneurship can include all of the following except:**
   a. The chance to keep your profits and make it big.
   b. Guaranteed success rates.
   c. The chance to see your dream become a reality.
   d. The opportunity to be your own boss.

3. **True or false: If your business idea fails, you shouldn't try again.**
   ○ True   ○ False

4. **To get your start-up off the ground, you'll need:**
   a. An idea, a team, and a product.
   b. A prototype, a distribution network, and a manufacturing plant.
   c. A really great pitch and a big check from your grandma.
   d. A lock of hair from Mark Zuckerberg, a tear from Elon Musk, and a voodoo doll.

5. **True or false: Getting your inspiration for a business model from an existing company is illegal.**

   ○ True   ○ False

6. **The process for launching a start-up includes:**
   a. A hot-dog-eating contest.
   b. Deciding whether to list your company's shares on the Nasdaq or the New York Stock Exchange.
   c. Researching the market and raising funds.
   d. Completing a Ninja Warrior obstacle course.

7. **A business plan is important for all of the following reasons except:**
   a. It's a legally binding contract between you and your company's investors.
   b. It can help you persuade investors to fund your idea.
   c. It can help you think through your idea.
   d. Measuring your progress against your business plan can help you stay on track.

8. **A business plan should be:**
   a. In iambic pentameter.
   b. As long or as short as you feel it should be.
   c. Filed with your state board of corporations.
   d. Written in Comic Sans, if you want anyone to take it seriously.

9. **True or false: A business plan can be written on the back of a napkin.**

   ○ True   ○ False

10. **Funding sources for a start-up can include all of the following, except:**
    a. Bootstrapping.
    b. Angels.
    c. Secondary offerings.
    d. Incubators.

11. **The benefits of raising outside funds for your start-up can include:**
    a. Greater access to funds and the chance to connect with mentors who can help you grow your business.
    b. Greater independence in how you run your business.
    c. Disappointing people outside your usual circle.
    d. The chance to finally live down that "Most likely to still be living with your parents at thirty" entry in your high school yearbook.

12. **The drawbacks to raising outside funds for your start-up can include:**
    a. Taking on a legal obligation to pay back equity investors if your company fails.
    b. Giving up ownership and control.
    c. Getting a few fingers chopped off if you fail.
    d. Having to explain to your investors why all the founders have Teslas even though you don't have any revenue yet.

13. **True or false: Holding an IPO is typically only an option for more established companies.**
    ○ True   ○ False

Answers

1. d	**5.** f	**9.** t	**13.** t
2. b	**6.** c	**10.** c	
3. f	**7.** a	**11.** a	
4. a	**8.** b	**12.** b	

9

Voodoo Economics

THE ECONOMY

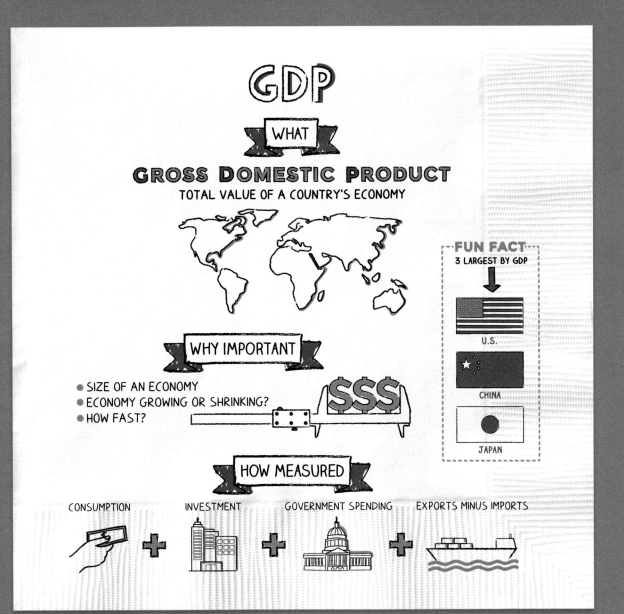

GDP

Gross domestic product, or GDP, measures the size of an economy. In essence, it puts a dollar sign on all the goods and services that a country produces in a given year (or other period).

Why Important

Tracking countries' GDPs tells us two things:

> › The overall size of a country's economy.
> › Whether the economy is growing or shrinking, and at what rate.

Investors, governments, and others watch GDP closely because it's generally considered the single best measure of how an economy is doing.

In good times, GDP should be increasing at a steady pace (that's called an expansion), workers are generally able to find jobs, corporations are turning profits, and typically, stocks are rising.

The opposite state of affairs is when the economy shrinks—called a recession. That can mean workers are losing their jobs and corporations are losing money. If unchecked, recessions can turn into economic death spirals (see: the Great Depression). Governments may watch GDP closely for any clues the economy could be headed for a recession, so that it can take steps to try to avoid or soften one.

How Measured

GDP includes four basic components:

> › Consumption—Just about everything you (and others) buy, such as a
>   new car, a sweater, or a bag of groceries, gets added to GDP.

- › Investment—This includes when a company builds a new factory or a homebuilder builds a new block of condos.
- › Government spending—This category includes everything from federal government spending on the military to a local government repaving a road.
- › Exports minus imports—If the country ships more goods and services abroad than it imports, this component is added to GDP. If the country imports more than it exports (called a trade deficit) then the difference is subtracted from GDP.

Fun Facts

- › At about $20 trillion, the U.S. is the world's largest economy, followed by China and Japan.
- › If California were a country it would rank as the fifth largest economy in the world—ahead of the U.K., India, and France.
- › GDP only includes over-the-table transactions. That means the illegal drug trade, prostitution, and your neighbor's under-the-table nanny's pay don't get counted.

Key Takeaways

- › GDP measures the size of an economy.
- › Investors watch GDP closely for signals as to how the economy is doing.
- › GDP includes goods and services that individuals, corporations, and the government buy but doesn't include black market or under-the-table activity.

The hair and makeup budgets for actresses attending the Oscars look like they surpass the combined GDPs of several small countries. —Napkin Finance ☺

INFLATION

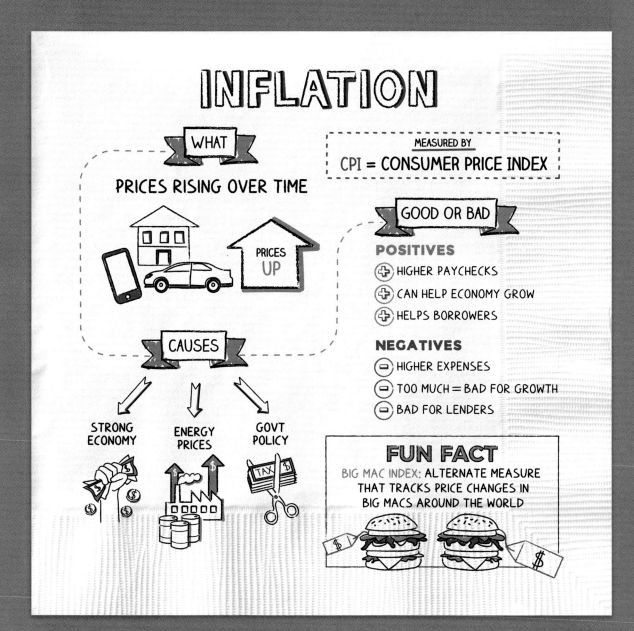

WHAT

PRICES RISING OVER TIME

PRICES UP

CAUSES

STRONG ECONOMY

ENERGY PRICES

GOVT POLICY

MEASURED BY

CPI = CONSUMER PRICE INDEX

GOOD OR BAD

POSITIVES

⊕ HIGHER PAYCHECKS

⊕ CAN HELP ECONOMY GROW

⊕ HELPS BORROWERS

NEGATIVES

⊖ HIGHER EXPENSES

⊖ TOO MUCH = BAD FOR GROWTH

⊖ BAD FOR LENDERS

FUN FACT

BIG MAC INDEX: ALTERNATE MEASURE THAT TRACKS PRICE CHANGES IN BIG MACS AROUND THE WORLD

Inflation

In 1980, you could buy a movie ticket for less than $3. These days, a ticket costs about $9 on average. The rise in prices over time is called inflation.

Why It Happens

Many different factors can contribute to inflation, including:

> *"Inflation is when you pay fifteen dollars for the ten-dollar haircut you used to get for five dollars when you had hair."*
>
> —SAM EWING, BASEBALL PLAYER

- › A booming economy—Economic growth usually goes hand in hand with at least some inflation. If a company's profits are good, it may give out more raises to employees. If people are feeling secure in their jobs, they're probably spending more money. The more they spend, the more prices tend to go up.
- › Energy prices—The economy depends on oil and other energy sources in a variety of ways. When the cost of energy goes up, the cost of making goods, shipping goods, and keeping the lights on at stores goes up too. That means prices of goods and services tend to rise as well.
- › Government policy—If the government cuts taxes, lowers interest rates, or prints money, both economic growth and inflation typically get a boost.

Good or Bad?

It might sound great to be able to buy a movie ticket for $3 or a house for $100,000, like you could in the 1980s. But some inflation helps grease the wheels of the economy. Plus, a little inflation is better than risking deflation (when prices fall), because deflation can pull an economy into a full-blown depression.

Government policy influences inflation (see Federal Reserve section later in this chapter). Many governments aim for around a 2% annual inflation rate—that's considered to be the sweet spot for slow but steady, positive inflation.

How Measured

The government tracks inflation with price indexes. Here's how it works:

Step 1: Economists put together a hypothetical basket of goods and services, which might represent what a typical family buys in a given period.

Step 2: Changes in the price for this basket of goods and services are tracked over time.

Step 3: The basket may be tweaked as people change what they buy, and its price may also be adjusted to account for improving quality (you don't pay more for a smartphone than a flip phone only because of inflation; you pay more because it's a more advanced product too).

In the U.S., the main measure of inflation is called the Consumer Price Index, or CPI.

Fun Facts

› One alternate measure of price changes is the Big Mac Index. You guessed it—it measures how the price of a Big Mac compares in different countries and changes over time.

› The CPI is incredibly controversial. Some experts argue that the way it's calculated tends to lowball inflation—which could help the government keep its costs down because some government payments rise with the inflation rate (such as Social Security payments).

Key Takeaways

› Inflation describes when prices in an economy rise over time.

› Although it may seem bad when things go up in price, a slow but steady rate of inflation is generally considered good for the economy.

› Economic growth, government policy, commodity prices, and other factors tend to influence the rate of inflation.

Inflation sucks because it means everyone is rich but nobody can afford anything. —Napkin Finance ☹

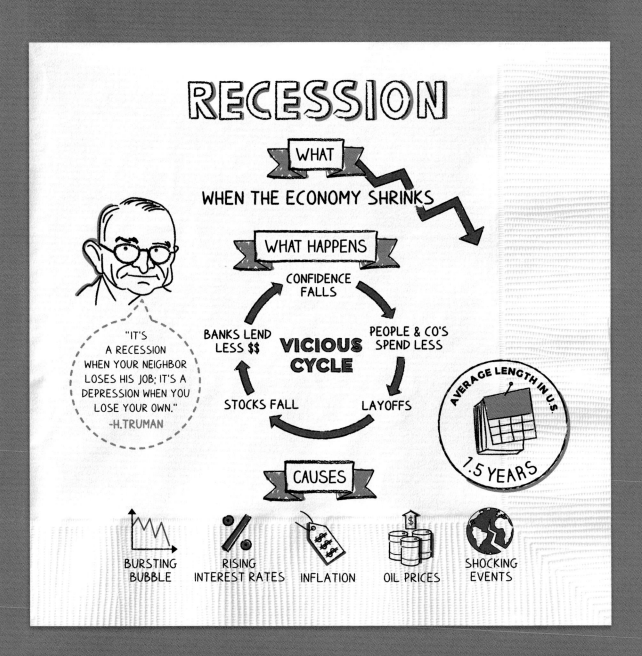

Recession

A recession refers to a time when the economy shrinks instead of grows. More specifically, economists typically define it as a time when GDP falls for at least two consecutive quarters.

What Happens

Recessions are economic downward spirals. Sometimes they can be fairly mild, and the economy (potentially with the help of the government) rights itself after only a few months. Sometimes they can be extreme. Here's how a recession typically plays out:

› Confidence declines—People and businesses start to worry about the economy. Since they're worried, they spend less money.
› Profits fall—As people and companies spend less, corporate profits fall or turn into losses.
› Workers lose their jobs—With profits falling, companies try to cut costs. This means layoffs.
› Stocks fall—If companies are earning less money, then their stocks are worth less. Falling stocks compound the problem—people and companies feel less rich (because their investments are worth less), meaning they spend even less money.
› Banks lend less money—With the economy heading south, banks start to worry that loans they make won't be paid back. Reduced lending also compounds the problem.

Causes

Recessions are complicated, and even experts disagree about their exact causes. Some causes that are at least partly to blame may include:

› Bursting bubbles
  › If a particular investment shoots way up in price—beyond what it's truly worth—then it's called a bubble. When the bubble pops, the investment's price falls fast and may pull other prices down with it.
› Rising interest rates
  › Higher interest rates hit the brakes on the economy.
› Inflation
  › Very high inflation makes it hard for the economy to run smoothly.
› Oil prices
  › Several historical recessions were at least partly caused by sudden spikes in the price of oil.
› Shocking events
  › The September 11 attacks likely contributed to the 2001 recession by disrupting the stock market and consumers' confidence.

How They End

The economy tends to move in cycles of growth and recessions. Recessions in the U.S. have always ended—often with the help of government policies to turn the economy around.

Fun Facts

› The average length of a recession in the U.S. is about a year and a half.
› More than 500 U.S. banks failed because of the Great Recession of

2007–09. About 7,000 failed during the Great Depression. (That's why we have FDIC insurance today.)

Key Takeaways

> › A recession is a time when the economy shrinks.
> › During a recession, confidence falls, profits fall, incomes fall, and unemployment rises.
> › Although a recession can look and feel awful when you're in the middle of it, U.S. recessions have always, eventually, ended.

With careful planning, hard work, and sharing a Netflix account with five other people, you can bounce back from a recession. —Napkin Finance ☺

The Fed

The Fed is the central bank of the U.S. Its overarching role is to make sure that the country's economy and financial system function smoothly.

Goals

The Fed has two official goals:

> › Maximizing sustainable employment
> › Supporting stable prices (i.e., regulating inflation) and moderate long-term interest rates

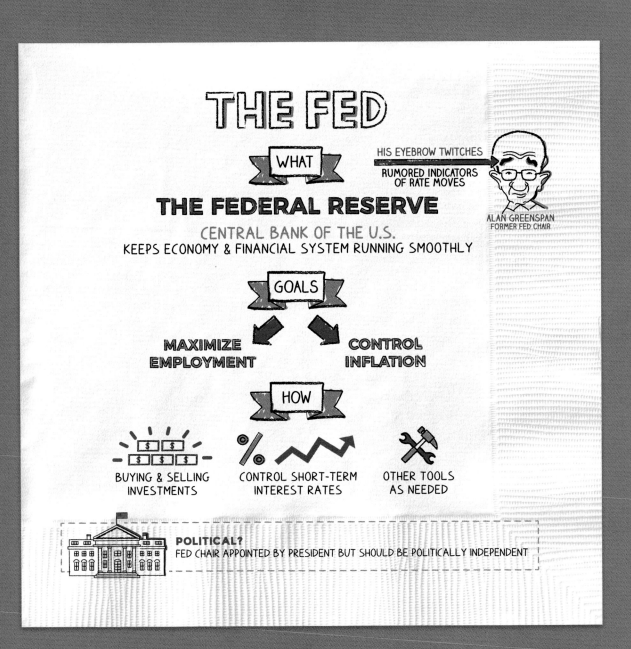

How Achieves

Here's what the Fed has in its toolbox:

What	How	Why
Interest rates	The Fed controls very short-term interest rates. Although it doesn't control the rate you pay for a mortgage or on your credit card, its actions affect these rates.	Lowering interest rates hits the gas on economic growth and inflation. Raising interest rates hits the brakes.
Market manipulation	The Fed can buy and sell U.S. government debt, and in some cases other investments.	By buying long-term debt, the Fed can lower long-term interest rates, which further boosts the economy. Buying securities has the effect of adding money to the economy—this is why people say the Fed "prints money." In response to the financial crisis of 2008–09, the Fed bought trillions of dollars of mortgage-backed securities to help stabilize the economy.
Improvising	If the economy's in a bind, the Fed may be able to come up with a creative way of helping.	During the financial crisis, the Fed also worked to prevent massive bank failures by helping orchestrate acquisitions (so failing banks could be purchased instead of going bankrupt).

Good to Know

Since the Fed may need to take actions that are unpopular with the party in power—such as by raising rates when the economy is overheating—it is supposed to be politically independent. However, the head of the Fed is appointed by the president, and it's not unheard of for a president to try to influence it.

Fun Facts

› It's true that the Fed metaphorically prints money, but it doesn't literally print money—the Treasury does.
› The stock market typically jumps when the Fed says (or hints) that it might cut rates and falls when it announces plans to hike rates. Vigilant traders used to scrutinize former fed chairman Alan Greenspan's every move—down to twitches in his eyebrows—for clues about what the Fed's next action might be.

Key Takeaways

› The Fed aims to keep the U.S. economy and financial system on track.
› The Fed controls some interest rates and may be able to affect the financial system in other ways, depending on the needs of the day.

The Federal Reserve is the regulator of the U.S. economy much like Tinder is the regulator of your love life. —Napkin Finance ☺

Chapter Quiz

1. **GDP stands for:**

   a. Growth of Demand for Products—meaning how many more goods and services the economy demanded compared with the previous year.

   b. Gross Domestic Product—meaning the total value of goods and services a country produces in a period of time.

   c. Gross Daily Profits—the average amount of profits earned in a given day in the economy.

   d. Government Doing Pranks—the name of the presidential cabinet's YouTube channel where they post their parkour videos.

2. **GDP is generally considered the single best measure of:**

   a. How the economy is doing.

   b. The level of inflation.

   c. Your return on investment for your English degree.

   d. How likely you are of Getting a Date to Prom.

3. **The components of GDP include all of the following, except:**

   a. Investment.

   b. Government spending.

   c. Transactions in the underground economy.

   d. Exports minus imports.

4. **True or false: China is the world's largest economy.**

   ○ True   ○ False

5. **Inflation is when:**

    a. The government exaggerates the level of GDP.

    b. Your Tinder date exaggerates his height.

    c. You eat too many burritos.

    d. Prices of goods and services rise over time.

6. **Inflation is:**

    a. Always bad because it means things cost more, so people buy less stuff.

    b. Good as long as it's slow and steady.

    c. Bad because you want to be able to wear heels on your dates.

    d. Another way to make you feel worthless.

7. **Deflation is:**

    a. What the Patriots did to those footballs.

    b. What your crush usually does to your ego.

    c. When economic growth turns negative.

    d. When prices of goods and services fall over time.

8. **A recession is a time when:**

    a. Economic growth turns negative.

    b. Unemployment falls.

    c. You're in between seasons of your favorite show.

    d. Your hair follicles say, "Peace out!"

9. **Some of the things that typically happen during a recession include all of the following except:**

    a. Stocks fall.

    b. Workers lose their jobs.

    c. The government shuts down.

    d. Banks lend less money.

10. **True or false: Recessions in the U.S. have always eventually ended.**

○ True ○ False

11. **The Federal Reserve is:**
    a. The central bank of the U.S.
    b. The primary issuer of currency in the U.S.
    c. A Nicolas Cage movie.
    d. Our nation's backup water supply.

12. **The Fed's main goal is to:**
    a. Make it seem like there's someone steering the boat.
    b. Maximize annual GDP growth.
    c. Maximize sustainable employment and regulate inflation.
    d. Get a selfie with Mark Zuckerberg.

13. **The main tools the Fed can use to accomplish its goals include:**
    a. Penalizing corporations that lay off workers during a recession.
    b. Raising or lowering short-term interest rates and buying and selling securities.
    c. Dropping bags of cash from the sky when the economy hits a rough patch.
    d. Allen wrenches from Ikea.

14. **True or false: The Fed is supposed to be politically independent because it may sometimes need to take actions that slow economic growth.**

○ True ○ False

Answers

1. b	**5.** d	**9.** c	**13.** b
2. a	**6.** b	**10.** t	**14.** t
3. c	**7.** d	**11.** a	
4. f	**8.** a	**12.** c	

The Bottom Line

BUSINESS

FINANCIAL STATEMENTS

WHAT

REPORTS ON COMPANY'S FINANCIAL HEALTH & PERFORMANCE

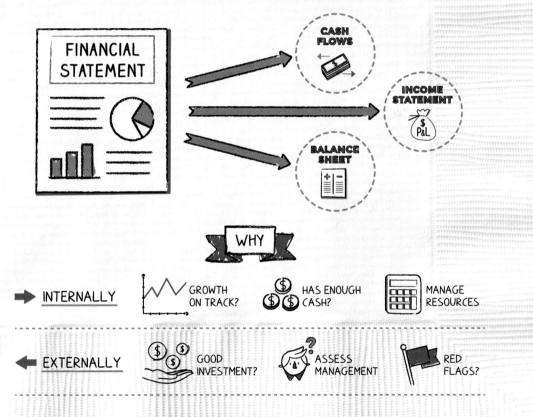

FINANCIAL STATEMENT

CASH FLOWS

INCOME STATEMENT
$ P&L

BALANCE SHEET

WHY

→ INTERNALLY — GROWTH ON TRACK? · HAS ENOUGH CASH? · MANAGE RESOURCES

← EXTERNALLY — GOOD INVESTMENT? · ASSESS MANAGEMENT · RED FLAGS?

Financial Statements

Financial statements are reports a company puts together to measure how it's doing.

Types

A company typically puts together three main statements:

What	Shows	Important because
Balance sheet	What the company owns and what it owes at a particular point in time.	Can show whether the company has the resources to meet its obligations.
Income statement, or "profit and loss"	Sales, expenses, and profits over a specific period of time, such as one year.	Trends in profits are hugely important to outside investors and to the company itself.
Statement of cash flows	Cash coming in and cash going out over a specific period of time.	Profits and cash measure different things, but both are important. For example, the cash-flow statement shows if customers are paying their bills.

Why Important

Financial statements are useful for the company itself, because they can show:

> › Which parts of the business are thriving and which are struggling.
> › Whether overall profits are shrinking or growing, and by how much.
> › Whether the company has enough cash to keep running smoothly.
> › Whether the company's debt load is reasonable.

Outside investors, regulators, and other users also use financial statements to:

› Determine whether to buy a company's stock, and to forecast future profits.
› Determine whether a company is likely to be able to pay back a loan.
› Try to make sure the company isn't fudging its accounting or doing anything nefarious.
› Figure out whether managers are making good decisions about which parts of the business to invest in.

Fun Facts

› One classic creative accounting trick is when a company erroneously classifies its routine business expenses as "investments." Doing so means it doesn't have to account for the expenses on its income statement, which inflates profits. (We're looking at you, WorldCom.)
› Accountants are in charge of counting ballots for the Oscars (and it was their fault when *La La Land* was mistakenly announced the Best Picture winner).

Key Takeaways

› Financial statements measure a company's financial performance.
› The main statements are the balance sheet, the profit and loss statement, and the statement of cash flows.

A financial statement is the business equivalent to "How you doin'?"
—Napkin Finance ☺

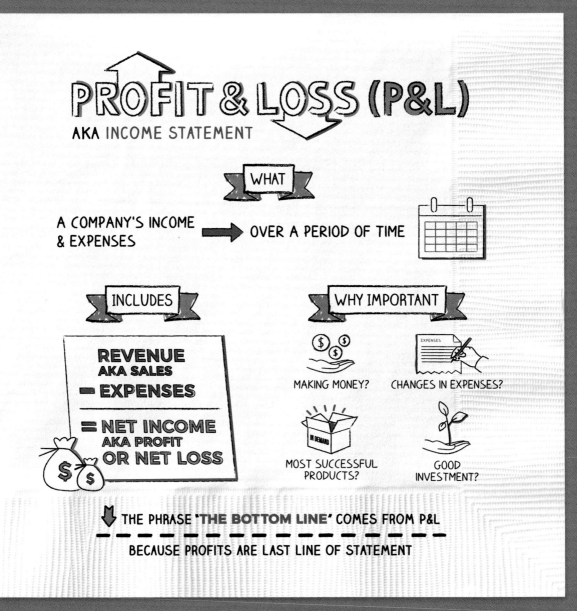

PROFIT & LOSS (P&L)

AKA INCOME STATEMENT

WHAT

A COMPANY'S INCOME & EXPENSES → OVER A PERIOD OF TIME

INCLUDES

REVENUE AKA SALES
− EXPENSES
= NET INCOME AKA PROFIT OR NET LOSS

WHY IMPORTANT

MAKING MONEY?

CHANGES IN EXPENSES?

MOST SUCCESSFUL PRODUCTS?

GOOD INVESTMENT?

THE PHRASE "**THE BOTTOM LINE**" COMES FROM P&L

BECAUSE PROFITS ARE LAST LINE OF STATEMENT

Profit & Loss (P&L)

A profit and loss statement, or income statement, shows the money a company earned and what it paid in expenses over a certain period.

The basic formula of the statement is:

Revenues (aka sales) - Expenses = Profits (aka net income or net loss)

What It Shows

Revenue, or sales, is straightforward: It puts a dollar figure on how much the company sold in its main business activities. For a clothing store, revenue would mean the total of all sales for the period (after any returns or discounts).

Expenses typically include a wide range of costs, including:

› The cost of what you sold—i.e., how much the store paid for those clothes it sold.
› Employee wages.
› The cost of rent, utilities, marketing, and other basic expenses of running the business.
› Depreciation—Suppose the store owns a truck. Every year the truck gets older and loses a bit of its value. That loss is factored in through depreciation.
› Interest payments on any debt.
› Taxes.

Why Important

> The main role of a profit and loss statement is to figure out whether or not the business made money in a given period, and how much it earned or lost.

> Looking at how profitable different parts of the business are can help the company improve its performance. For example, if the clothing store is earning a 25% profit on jewelry but only 10% on jeans, and jewelry is selling better, it may decide to carry more jewelry and fewer jeans.

> Prospective investors may want to see statements for several past periods before forking over their money.

Fun Facts

> Tesla has never earned an annual profit, yet the company is worth tens of billions of dollars. (But it's only worth that much because investors believe that one day it will earn plenty of profits.)

> A $6,000 gold-and-burgundy shower curtain was among the expenses former Tyco CEO Dennis Kozlowski fraudulently claimed as a company expense, before he went to prison.

Key Takeaways

> A profit and loss statement shows what a company's sales, expenses, and profits were for a given period.

> The statement can provide valuable information for the company itself, in making decisions about how to run the business, and also for potential outside investors.

Better to have profited and lost than never to have profited at all. —Napkin Finance ☺

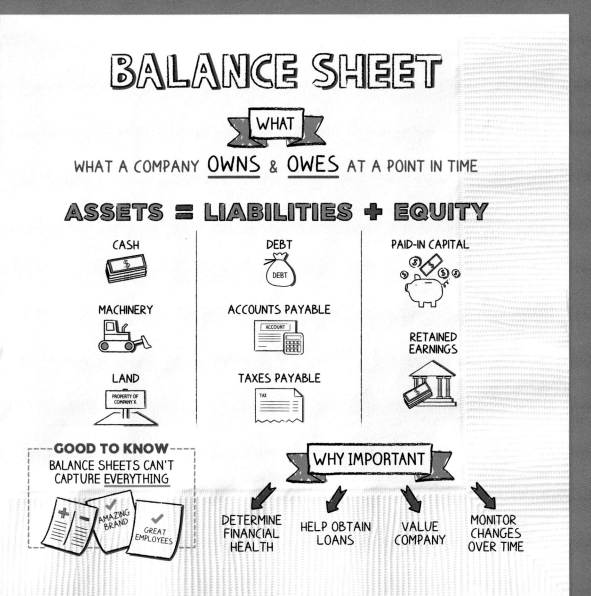

Balance Sheet

A balance sheet is a snapshot of financial health, showing what a company or person owns and owes at a specific point in time.

The Basics

Balance sheets always follow the same formula:

$$Assets = Liabilities + Equity$$

An asset can be anything that provides or will provide a benefit. A liability is an obligation that will require the company (or you) to spend resources in the future. Equity means ownership, and it's what's left of the assets after subtracting the liabilities.

What's Included

A company's balance sheet might show some of these items:

Assets	Liabilities	Equity
Cash and investments	Debt	Paid-in capital (i.e., what owners have paid into the company)
Accounts receivable	Accounts payable	
Inventory	Salaries payable	Retained earnings (i.e., accumulated profits)
Machinery	Taxes payable	
Land	Unearned revenue	

How Used

Investors may use the balance sheet to:

> › Figure out what the company's shares are worth.
> › Evaluate whether the company is in good financial health.

Lenders may use the balance sheet to:

> › Decide whether they should loan new money to the company.
> › Work out whether the company is likely to repay the money it's already borrowed.

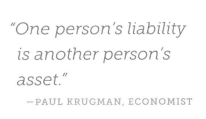

"One person's liability is another person's asset."

—PAUL KRUGMAN, ECONOMIST

Company insiders may use the balance sheet to:

> › Make sure it has enough cash handy to meet upcoming expenses.
> › See how its assets and liabilities have changed since the last year.

Fun Facts

> › Balance sheets can't always capture the entire picture. For example, companies can't count having an amazing brand or terrific employees as assets, even though these can provide substantial benefits.
> › The phrase "cook the books" doesn't come from any real-world case of culinary accounting fraud. Rather, it comes from one meaning of the word *cook* as to alter or modify something.

Balance sheets would be way more popular if they came in 1,000-thread
count. —Napkin Finance ☺

Liability

A liability is something that will require you (or a company) to spend money or resources
in the future. For example, your student loans are a liability because you have to pay
them off.

Types

Companies and people can have a range of liabilities:

Business	Personal
Bonds	Credit card debt
Money owed to suppliers	Student loans
Money owed to employees	Mortgages
Taxes	Unpaid bills
Pension payments for retirees	Anything you've promised to do in the future

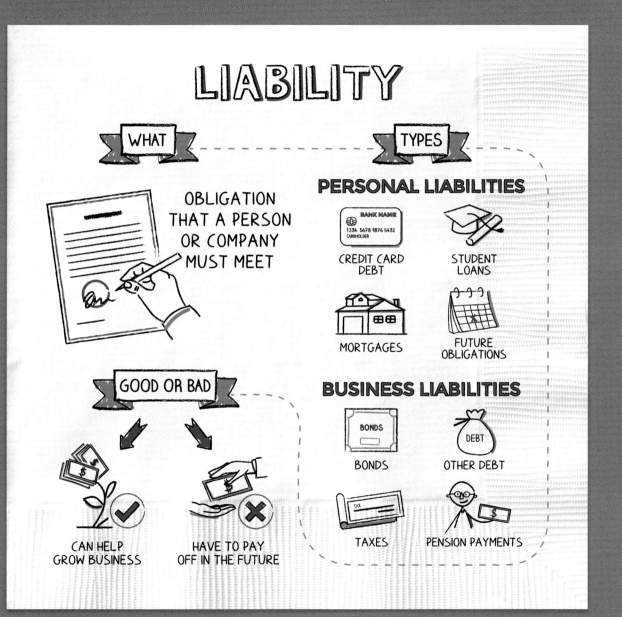

Good or Bad?

Although the word *liability* sounds bad (like the way your cranky uncle is a liability at the Thanksgiving dinner table), taking on liabilities can be helpful. If you take on student loans so you can go to college, there's a good chance you'll end up earning more money as a result.

If a company takes on debt to grow its business, it can end up financially stronger. And if the company has liabilities because it owes taxes on its profits, or owes money to its employees because business has been booming, then those liabilities aren't necessarily bad things.

Liabilities can help predict outflows of money in the future—but on their own, higher liabilities aren't necessarily good or bad.

Fun Facts

› Receiving money can create a liability. If a company is paid in advance, it has to create a liability for unearned revenue (since it owes the customer something).

› Another classic accounting trick is when a company creates a separate legal entity to buy its bad assets or take on extra debt on its behalf. If the new entity is legally distinct, the parent company may not have to share details in its financial statements. (We're looking at you, Enron.)

Key Takeaways

› A liability is something that you, or another person or company, will have to spend money or effort on in the future.

› Any kind of debt generally counts as a liability, and so can promises of future services.

> › Although liabilities can represent owed money, higher liabilities aren't necessarily a bad thing.

Some examples of liabilities are debt, lawsuits, and a hammered wedding guest. —Napkin Finance 😶

Chapter Quiz

1. **Companies may use their financial statements internally to:**
   a. Find out who has been stealing reams of paper.
   b. Figure out how much toilet paper they go through every month.
   c. Figure out which type of accounting fraud they have the best chance of getting away with using.
   d. Figure out which products and services are selling best.

2. **Outsiders may use a company's financial statements to:**
   a. Steal its identity and claim its tax refund.
   b. Rank its board for hotness.
   c. Find its weak spot and destroy it like the Death Star.
   d. Decide whether or not to make an investment.

3. **The main financial statements include all of the following except:**
   a. Balance sheet.
   b. Profit and liabilities statement.
   c. Cash-flow statement.
   d. Income statement.

4. **True or false: The profit and loss and income statement are the same thing.**

   ○ True   ○ False

5. **The basic formula of the profit and loss statement is:**

   a. Revenue - Expenses = Profits.
   b. Assets = Liabilities + Equity.
   c. Money = Happiness.
   d. Old Bitcoin Purchases + Google IPO Shares = Yacht.

6. **Expenses can include:**

   a. Hours of useless office small talk you'll never get back.
   b. Office Fantasy Football losses.
   c. Wages to employees and the cost of what you sold.
   d. Dividends to shareholders.

7. **True or false: For a company's stock to be worth anything, it must be profitable.**

   ○ True   ○ False

8. **The balance sheet shows:**

   a. Inflows and outflows over a specific period of time.
   b. What a company owns and owes at a specific point in time.
   c. What the company paid out in expenses over the last year.
   d. A company's pH balance.

9. **Types of assets can include all of the following except:**

   a. Cash.
   b. Machinery.
   c. Average education level of employees.
   d. Land.

10. **True or false: Equity, or ownership, is what's left of a company's assets after you subtract for its liabilities.**

   ○ True   ○ False

11. **Business liabilities can include:**

   a. Cost of goods sold.
   b. Mandatory conversations with employees' spouses at company functions.
   c. Sriracha expenses for millennial employees.
   d. Money owed to suppliers, employees, and others.

12. **Personal liabilities can include:**

   a. Your credit card debt and your student loans.
   b. Your 401(k) contributions and your automatic transfers to your savings account.
   c. An inability not to text your ex when inebriated.
   d. Forgetting to clear your browser history.

13. **True or false: Receiving money for work a company hasn't completed yet creates a liability.**

   ○ True   ○ False

Answers

1. d	**5.** a	**9.** c	**13.** t
2. d	**6.** c	**10.** t	
3. b	**7.** f	**11.** d	
4. t	**8.** b	**12.** a	

11

The Future of Money

CRYPTOCURRENCY

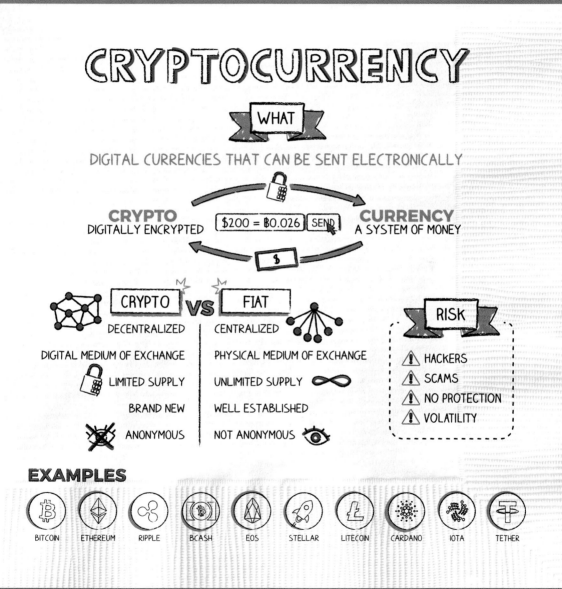

Cryptocurrency

Cryptocurrency is digital money that can be sent electronically anywhere in the world.

Crypto vs. Traditional Currency

Cryptocurrency is a system that relies on sophisticated encryption (hence the name) and a network of online users to function—compared with traditional currency, which is backed by a government. Here is what that difference really means:

Crypto	Fiat/traditional
Decentralized—no one person, government, or corporation controls cryptocurrency.	Centralized—traditional currencies are issued and regulated by government entities.
Digital—cryptocurrency only exists online and can only be traded online (although some companies will happily sell you souvenirs they describe as physical Bitcoins).	Physical—traditional money can exist digitally, as in your bank account, but can also exist as physical bills and coins.
Limited supply—crypto is typically created with a finite supply. That could help it hold its value over time.	Unlimited supply—governments can always print more money, which can make fiat currency lose value to inflation.
Anonymous—crypto transactions can't be traced back to real humans.	Not anonymous—traditional transactions generally can be tracked.
Brand new—the first cryptocurrency, Bitcoin, was launched in 2009.	Well established—mainstream currency has been around for eons.

Quick Riches, Big Risks

Cryptocurrency is an exciting but controversial part of the world of finance.

Some investors have become millionaires almost overnight as the currencies have taken off in value. But with the potential for great returns comes the possibility of great losses. The risks of investing in cryptocurrency include:

> *"Virtual currencies . . . may hold long-term promise, particularly if the innovations promote a faster, more secure, and more efficient payment system."*
>
> —BEN BERNANKE, FORMER FED CHAIR

> › Hackers—Digital wallets, where cryptocurrency is stored, can be vulnerable to hacking.
> › Scams—Fraudsters may advertise a fake new cryptocurrency then disappear overnight.
> › No protection—If your crypto disappears or goes to $0 tomorrow, there may not be anything you can do.
> › Volatility—Cryptocurrency prices can swing from $0 to the thousands and back again in the blink of an eye. They make the stock market look tame.

Fun Facts

> › More than 2,000 types of cryptocurrency existed as of 2019, with a total combined value of more than $100 billion.
> › Newly minted cryptomillionaires have something else in common: They love Magic: The Gathering cards. Prices of the highest-value Magic cards have jumped tenfold in recent years due to interest from cryptocurrency investors.

› Looking for another way to blow your cryptofortune? Try CryptoKitties—a Blockchain-based game for collecting and selling digital cats. A single CryptoKitty has sold for as much as $170,000.

Key Takeaways

› Cryptocurrency is digital money that exists online through a network of users.
› Unlike traditional currencies, crypto isn't controlled by a central government or other entity.
› Some cryptocurrency investors have gotten rich quick, but there are major risks to investing.

Cryptocurrencies can't be counterfeited, unlike a Birkin bag sold out of a trunk. —Napkin Finance ☺

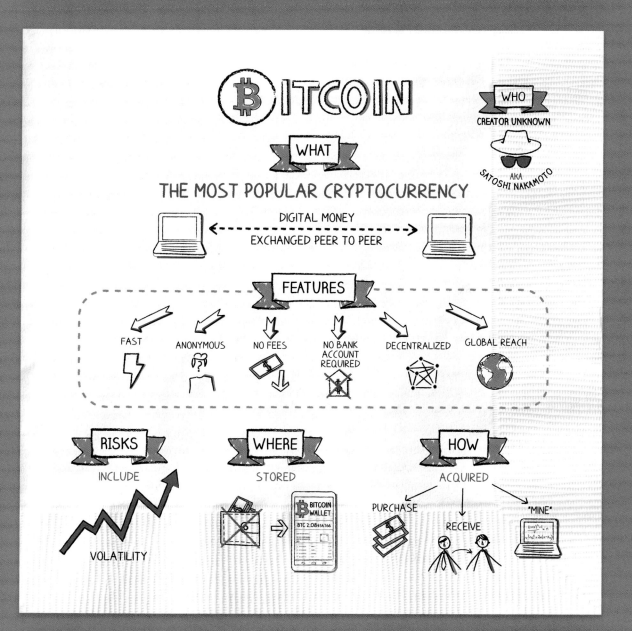

Bitcoin

Bitcoin is the world's first, and arguably most successful, cryptocurrency.

Path to Success

2008: The world economy is a mess, and faith in the traditional financial system is low. An author calling himself Satoshi Nakamoto, but whose real name is unknown, releases a paper explaining how a digital peer-to-peer currency could work.

2009: Satoshi mines the first block of Bitcoin—equivalent to the first bills of a new currency being printed. The first Bitcoin-to-dollars exchange rate is set, which allows the first purchases of Bitcoins to take place.

2010: A man in Florida pays for two pizzas with 10,000 Bitcoins—the first physical purchase using the currency.

2012–13: The price of one Bitcoin crosses $100, and then $1,000.

2014–18: Bitcoin goes mainstream. It becomes an accepted form of payment with PayPal and some other major businesses. By 2018, one in twenty Americans owns some.

> *"Bitcoin will do to banks what email did to the postal industry."*
>
> —RICK FALKVINGE, TECH PROVOCATEUR

How to Acquire

There are three ways to acquire Bitcoin:

> › Purchase—You can buy Bitcoin with
> another currency, such as dollars,
> just like you can trade dollars for
> Euros or other traditional currencies.
> › Receive—You can trade goods or
> services for Bitcoin.
> › Mine—You can become a
> Bitcoin miner, which is someone
> who devotes a large amount
> of computing power to solving
> complex math problems, and gets rewarded in Bitcoin.

"It's gold for nerds."

—STEPHEN COLBERT,
ENTERTAINER

High Highs, Low Lows

Bitcoin may be the most established cryptocurrency, but it's far from tame. In its short lifetime, its price has gone from a low of less than $0.01 per coin to almost $20,000, before losing more than 80% of its value.

Fun Facts

> › That Florida pizza buyer's Bitcoin (as mentioned above) would have
> eventually been worth more than $20 million if he'd held on to them.
> › One unlucky man from Wales lost more than $100 million in Bitcoin
> when he threw away his computer hard drive. The device is now buried
> in a landfill near his home.

> The Winklevoss twins (of *The Social Network* fame) reportedly have enough invested in Bitcoin that at one point in time they were Bitcoin billionaires. (That was before the price of Bitcoin took a big fall.)

Key Takeaways

> Bitcoin is the first and most well established cryptocurrency.
> Although you can now use Bitcoin with some major businesses, it's still not widely accepted, and the price can swing wildly.
> You can acquire Bitcoin by buying, receiving, or mining it.

Nothing is more fun than hearing someone who just learned about Bitcoin explain it to someone who's never heard of it. —Napkin Finance ☺

Initial Coin Offering

An ICO, or Initial Coin Offering, is a way for companies to raise money by inventing and issuing a new type of digital money. Normally, early investors become partial owners of a company (such as by investing in its IPO). With an ICO, investors receive a new currency instead, which could end up being worth a lot of real money or could turn out to be worthless.

How It Works

During an ICO campaign:

> "Tokens" are sold by a company during an initial offering.
> Supporters buy these tokens, usually in exchange for a well-established virtual currency, such as Ethereum or Bitcoin.

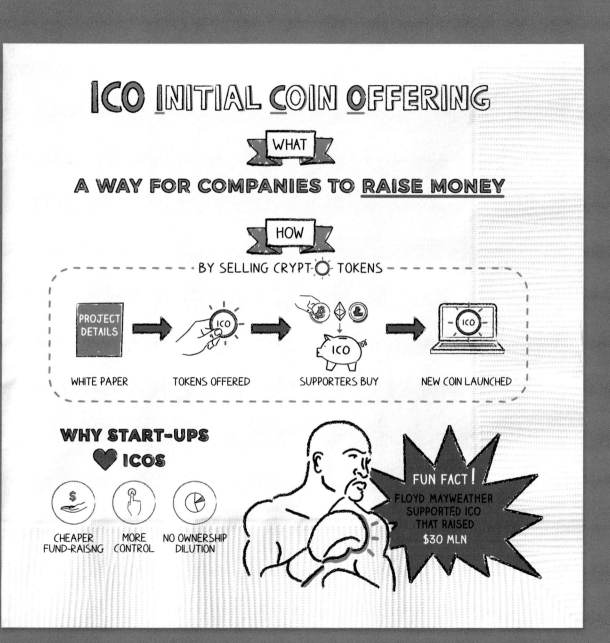

> If the money raised meets the minimum amount needed within the set time frame, the tokens convert into the new form of cryptocurrency.
> If the money raised does not meet the minimum amount set, funds are typically returned to investors.

Why Start-Ups Love ICOs

ICOs offer many benefits for the companies that use them, including:

> Cheaper fund-raising—It's easier and cheaper for companies to hold an ICO rather than an IPO.
> No ownership dilution—When a company sells shares, the original owners see their ownership positions reduced. With an ICO, existing owners hold on to what they have.
> More control—When a venture capital firm invests in a start-up, the firm typically gains a say in the company's business. With an ICO, founders can keep more control.

Pros and Cons for Investors

Pros	Cons
Chance to get in on the ground floor of a successful start-up	Poor disclosures
Backers may enjoy being part of a disruptive movement	Lack of regulation
Possibility of making a lot of money	May have difficulty exiting an investment
	Risk of hackers stealing funds
	Value of tokens can fluctuate wildly
	Risk of outright scams

Fun Facts

› Athletes and celebrities are jumping on the ICO bandwagon. Floyd Mayweather, Jr., promoted an ICO for a Blockchain-based prediction market that raised $30 million.

› CannabisCoin, Catcoin, Sexcoin, and WhopperCoin are all real cryptocurrencies. With enough WhopperCoin, you can get a free burger at a Burger King in Russia.

Key Takeaways

› An ICO—a play on *IPO*—is a way of raising funds by creating a new cryptocurrency.

› ICOs offer great benefits for companies, including cheaper fund-raising and more control, but can pose significant risks for investors.

The difference between an ICO and Monopoly money is that Monopoly money is recyclable. —Napkin Finance ☹

Blockchain

Blockchain is the innovative technology that Bitcoin and some other cryptocurrencies are built on. Although the mechanics of Blockchain can be difficult to understand, its big innovation is creating a permanent record that can't be changed or destroyed. That could make it useful in applications far beyond cryptocurrency.

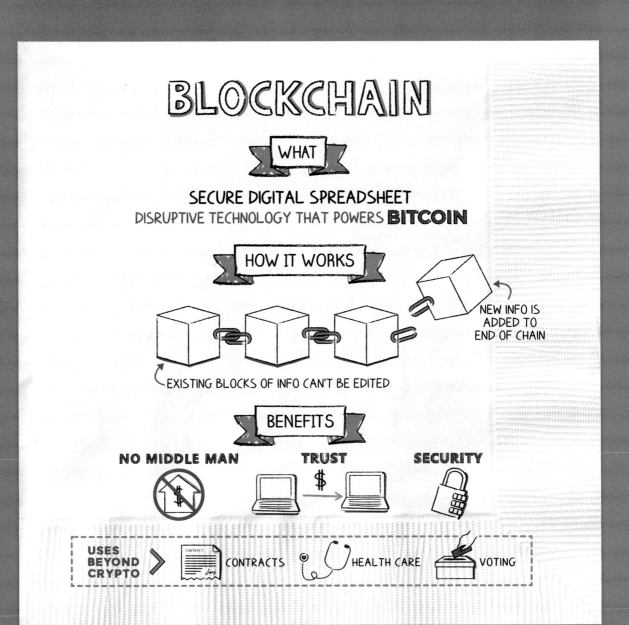

How It Works

Blockchain is like a huge, public spreadsheet. But unlike something you create in Excel, once an entry is made in the Blockchain it is essentially unchangeable. That's because the spreadsheet is encrypted and spread out over a wide network of users.

Instead of being able to edit existing entries, new entries are always added to the end of the chain (in "blocks"). And each block is connected to the one before it through a series of numbers. What you end up with is an unchangeable history of information.

Benefits

The big advantages of Blockchain are:

> *"Blockchains are record-keeping backed by fancy math."*
> —EDWARD SNOWDEN, FORMER GOVERNMENT CONTRACTOR AND INTERNATIONAL FUGITIVE

› Trust. If a record can't be edited (for example, the bank can't accidentally erase a zero from the end of your account) then you can trust it.

› No middle man. Because the Blockchain is spread over a wide network, there's no central person or group controlling the flow of information (or money).

› Security. Because the information is encrypted and decentralized, it's essentially impossible for one person or organized group of people to hack it.

Beyond Crypto

Blockchain has the potential to disrupt countless other industries, including:

> › Contracts—Whether transferring real estate or entering into a business contract, with Blockchain technology, all previously agreed-to terms could be public and verifiable, but also secure.
> › Health care—Medical providers could use the technology to share sensitive information in an efficient, secure way.
> › Voting—Blockchain could serve as a secure, anonymous, but verifiable technology for tallying votes.

Fun Facts

> › Blockchain-powered Bitcoin uses more energy than 159 individual countries, due to the energy-intensiveness of mining for new coin.
> › The musician Imogen Heap is using Blockchain to try to build a "fair trade" system for music, so artists can receive adequate pay for their work.

Key Takeaways

> › Blockchain is the technology that powers Bitcoin and other cryptocurrencies.
> › The big innovation of Blockchain has been to create a system of record keeping that can't be tampered with.
> › Although it's mainly used for cryptocurrency, Blockchain has the potential to be used in voting, contracts, the music industry, and more.

Blockchain is disruptive technology that powers Bitcoin, while the iPhone is disruptive technology that powers procrastination. —Napkin Finance ☺

Chapter Quiz

1. **Cryptocurrency is:**
   a. A type of tax-free account you can use to fund your future burial expenses.
   b. Electronic Monopoly money.
   c. Digital currency that's encrypted.
   d. The only type of currency that's accepted in the Burning Man "gift economy."

2. **The differences between cryptocurrency and traditional currency include all of the following except:**
   a. The value of traditional currency is guaranteed against inflation while that of cryptocurrency is not.
   b. Traditional currency is backed by a government while cryptocurrency is not.
   c. You can't make it rain with cryptocurrency.
   d. Old white presidents' faces.

3. **The risks of investing in cryptocurrency include:**
   a. Being too interesting at parties.
   b. A robot uprising.
   c. The possibility of the government confiscating your cryptocurrency.
   d. Big price swings.

4. **True or false: There are more than two thousand types of cryptocurrency.**
   ○ True   ○ False

5. **The process for creating new units of Bitcoin is called:**
   a. Mining.
   b. Minting.
   c. Musking.
   d. Getting Bit AF.

6. **True or false: Bitcoin is considered the most established cryptocurrency because its price is very stable.**

   ○ True   ○ False

7. **True or false: Because Bitcoin is a digital-only currency, you can't use it to buy goods or services with any traditional businesses.**

   ○ True   ○ False

8. **An initial coin offering, or ICO, is:**

   a. A surefire way to invest 100% of your retirement savings.
   b. A type of fund-raising option for companies.
   c. When QVC sells commemorative coins.
   d. Elon Musk's pickup line.

9. **ICOs can be great deals for the companies that use them because:**

   a. The companies are guaranteed a minimum level of fund-raising.
   b. The federal government regulates them heavily.
   c. Companies generally don't have to give up any ownership or control.
   d. They come with a free tote bag.

10. **The basic trade-off for investors of buying into an ICO is:**

    a. Whether to invest their gains in the stock market or in more ICOs.
    b. Whether to buy a Model S or Model X Tesla with their profits.
    c. Whether to diversify among different ICOs or make a concentrated bet on just one.
    d. The chance to make a lot of money versus the chance of losing all their invested money.

11. **Blockchain is:**

   a. Disruptive record-keeping technology that powers Bitcoin.
   b. A chain of computers used to mine for Bitcoin.
   c. An old video rental company.
   d. An impenetrable fence that Silicon Valley is building around itself before it declares itself an independent country.

12. **The big innovation of Blockchain is:**

   a. Creating artificially intelligent robots that can defraud the government.
   b. Creating a highly secure way of storing information.
   c. Creating VR bankruptcy.
   d. Creating an opportunity for computer geeks everywhere to finally move out of their moms' basements.

13. **True or false: Blockchain could have potential applications far beyond cryptocurrency.**

   ◯ True   ◯ False

14. **True or false: Blockchain is also highly environmentally efficient.**

   ◯ True   ◯ False

Answers

1. c	**5.** a	**9.** c	**13.** t
2. a	**6.** f	**10.** d	**14.** f
3. d	**7.** f	**11.** a	
4. t	**8.** b	**12.** b	

12

Wow Your Friends

COCKTAIL PARTY TOPICS

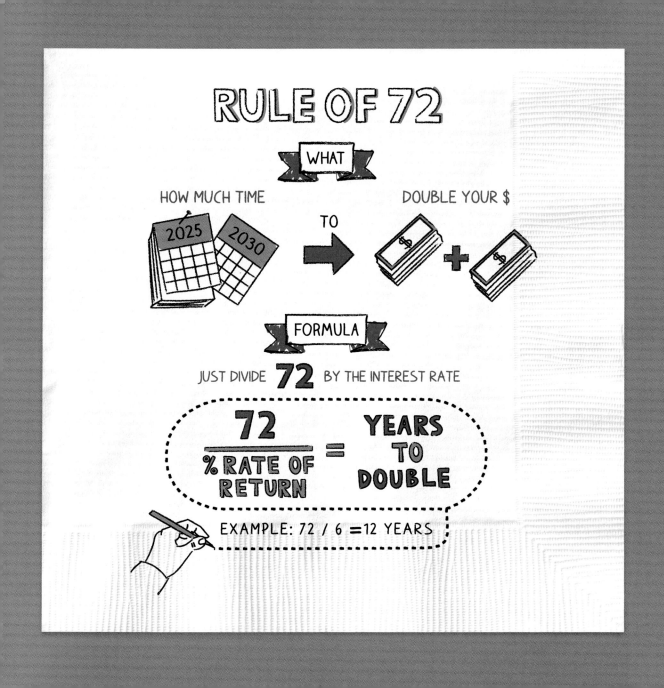

Rule of 72

The rule of 72 is an easy, back-of-the-napkin way to figure out how long it will take invested money to double, given a set interest rate or growth rate.

How It Works

To use the rule, just divide the number 72 by your annual interest rate.

So, if your money is earning 7% every year, it will double in about:

72/7 = 10.3 years.

If your money is earning 2% every year, it will double in about:

72/2 = 36 years (ouch).

What It Is and What It Isn't

The rule of 72 is an easy way to estimate your money's growth, but it isn't a precise calculation. The math for working out the exact length of time is quite a bit more complicated (though online calculators can help). Plus, in the real world, return rates aren't usually smooth from year to year (or from decade to decade).

Tips

As you learned in elementary school, putting a larger number in the denominator means your result gets smaller. It may not be a shocking revelation, but one of the best ways to help your money double faster (and then double again!) is to seek out a higher rate of return. You can help along your money's growth by:

> › Investing money you won't need for a long time in stocks. With 10% historical returns, stocks have on average doubled investors' money about every seven years.

›   Avoiding accounts that don't yield anything. Don't keep any more cash than you have to in a 0% checking account. Even your emergency fund could live in a high-yield savings account.

›   Leaving your money to grow. The rule of 72 assumes compound growth. If you withdraw the money you've earned every year and spend it, your money will never double.

Fun Facts

›   Although Einstein is often credited with discovering the rule of 72, it was more likely discovered by an Italian mathematician named Luca Pacioli in the late 1400s. Pacioli also invented modern accounting.

›   To find out how long it will take for your money to triple, divide 114 by your interest rate. And to find out how long it will take to quadruple, use 144.

Key Takeaways

›   The rule of 72 is a quick and easy way to figure out roughly how long it will take your money to double at a given growth rate.

›   To help your money double faster, try to seek out higher growth rates, such as by investing in stocks, and make sure you leave your money to grow instead of withdrawing it.

The rule of 72 is a shortcut to compounding, while eating doughnuts is a shortcut to cellulite. —Napkin Finance ☺

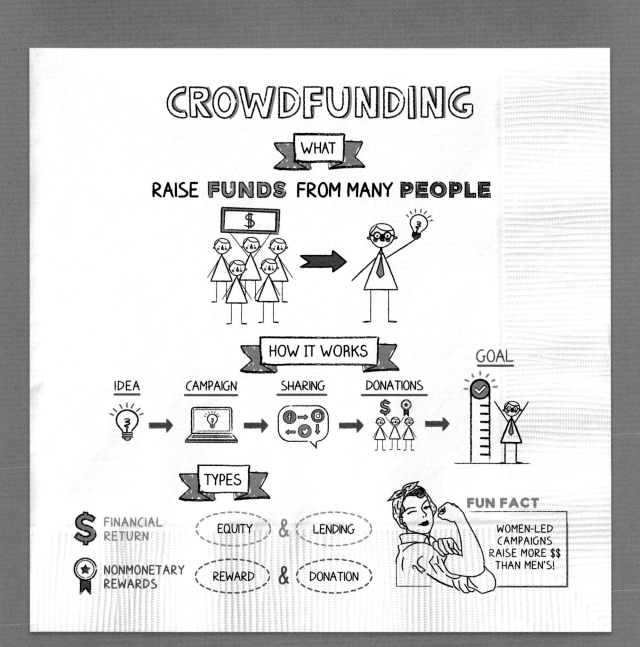

Crowdfunding

Crowdfunding is a way to raise money from many people, thanks to the power of the Internet. Crowdfunding websites such as Kickstarter are platforms you can use to advertise the idea you're hoping to fund and to receive donations.

How It Works

A typical crowdfunding campaign looks something like this:

Step 1: Have an idea. It could be something you've already been working toward or a completely new concept.

Step 2: Figure out how much money you would need to make your idea a reality. That number will be your fundraising goal.

Step 3: Choose a crowdfunding website. (See the table on the following page for a list of some of the major players.)

Step 4: Write up your pitch. Ask some friends to help you create a compelling story that will get some clicks.

Step 5: Launch your campaign.

Step 6: Promote your campaign through social media and any way you can. Try to reach as many people as possible! Go viral!

Step 7: Rake in those donations and (hopefully) hit or exceed your fundraising goal.

Step 8: Bring your idea to life.

Types

	What	Examples
Donations	Donate money to someone needy, and expect nothing in return.	GoFundMe, CrowdRise
Rewards	Give $20 to an entrepreneur trying to develop a product, and in exchange, be one of the first to receive the product once it's developed.	Kickstarter, Indiegogo
Equity	Like buying a stock, invest some money in a new company and receive a fractional ownership stake.	SeedInvest, Wefunder
Loans	Lend money to someone who needs it, and get paid back over time with interest.	LendingClub, Prosper

Pros and Cons

	Pros	Cons
For fund-raisers	Simple and easy Potential to reach a wide audience	At first, you're asking for money from people you know (awkward) No guarantee you'll reach your goal
For donors/ investors	Help a real human instead of a faceless organization Get in on the ground floor of something cool	Not much protection; scams can happen Donations often not tax-deductible

Fun Facts

› Half-baked business plans that nevertheless received thousands of dollars in funding on Kickstarter have included: making potato salad, shooting a *Doctor Who*–style police box into orbit, and sending an inflated Lionel Richie head on a trip around the world.

› Female-led crowdfunding campaigns tend to raise more money than those backed by men, possibly because women are seen as more trustworthy.

Key Takeaways

› Crowdfunding is a way to raise large amounts of money through small contributions on the Internet.

› Crowdfunding can be used to solicit charitable donations or funds to get a new business off the ground.

› Although crowdfunding can be easy and convenient for both fund-raisers and donors, it offers few protections or guarantees for either side.

Hosting a potluck is a great way to crowdfund your dinner party.
—Napkin Finance ☺

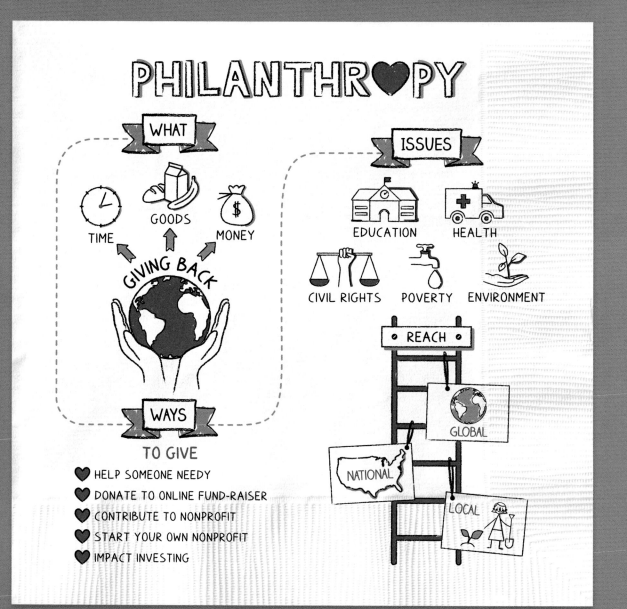

Philanthropy

Philanthropy is giving back. It's paying forward the resources you have—whether your money, or physical goods, or time and effort—to help someone in need. Some people may get into philanthropy for the tax breaks, while others find it gives meaning to their lives and lets them connect with other people.

> *"To move forward, you have to give something back."*
> —OPRAH WINFREY, #BOSS

Ways to Give

There are many ways to help, including:

> › Helping a needy person in your area.
> › Donating to an online fund-raiser.
> › Contributing money, canned goods, other belongings, or your time to a nonprofit.
> › Creating your own nonprofit to tackle a challenge no one else is working on.
> › Engaging in impact investing—putting your money to work in a way that should help it grow, but also help society or the planet.

Issues

You can give to an organization that specializes in a particular challenge, such as:

> › Civil rights.
> › Education.
> › The environment.
> › Health.
> › Poverty.

You can also consider what kind of geographic reach you want your giving to have, such as:

> › Local—Help someone needy in your own backyard, or volunteer at a local soup kitchen.
> › National—Contribute to victims of a natural disaster, donate to a medical research organization, or work to protect conservation lands in the U.S.
> › Global—Donate to help some of the world's neediest. Help bring medical care to war zones, food to refugees, or education to children living in poverty.

"I've always respected those who tried to change the world for the better, rather than just complain about it."

—MICHAEL BLOOMBERG, BUSINESSMAN AND POLITICIAN

Good to Know

If you're in it for the tax breaks, there are rules you need to know. Donations to individuals—whether in real life or through crowdfunding—generally aren't deductible. And you have to itemize your deductions in order to claim a benefit.

Fun Facts

› The Giving Pledge is a pact—started by Warren Buffett and Bill and Melinda Gates—among many of the world's billionaires to give away most of their fortunes. Almost two hundred people from around the world have signed on.

› Women are more likely to donate to charity than men, and on average donate more money when they do than men.

› Some companies engage in giving-through-commerce. Prescription-glasses retailer Warby Parker and shoe company Toms each give away one pair of their product for every one that's purchased.

Key Takeaways

› Philanthropy is taking whatever resources you have in life—whether money, time, or expertise—and paying it forward.

› There are many ways to give, depending on what you have to contribute and what kind of an impact you want to make.

› Giving can provide tax breaks, but there are rules and restrictions to claiming a deduction.

Sorry, but "liking" a picture of people helping out at a soup kitchen doesn't count as philanthropy. —Napkin Finance ☺

Hedge Funds

Hedge funds—like mutual funds—pool investors' money and hire one or more professional managers to buy and sell investments. Unlike mutual funds, hedge funds are lightly regulated and often high risk. You can think of them as mutual funds on steroids.

Hedge Funds vs. Mutual Funds

The main thing that hedge funds and mutual funds have in common is that (not surprisingly) both are funds. Their differences, however, are many:

	Hedge funds	Mutual funds
Who can invest?	Only the wealthy (regulators set a certain minimum level of assets or income).	Anyone.
What can they invest in?	Almost anything—from traditional stocks and bonds, to derivatives, to life insurance contracts.	There are strict legal limits on what they can invest in, and most stick to vanilla stocks and bonds.
Do you know what your fund owns?	Not necessarily. Hedge funds don't have to tell investors (or the government) much about what they're investing in.	Yes. Mutual funds have to file periodic reports in which they detail every single investment that they own.
How expensive are they?	Very. A typical fee structure is 2% of all money invested plus 20% of profits.	Moderately. The average fee for mutual funds is about 0.5% of assets per year.
Is it easy to exit an investment?	No. There are generally strict restrictions on when investors can (and can't) withdraw funds.	Yes. Investors can generally redeem mutual fund shares on any day the market's open.

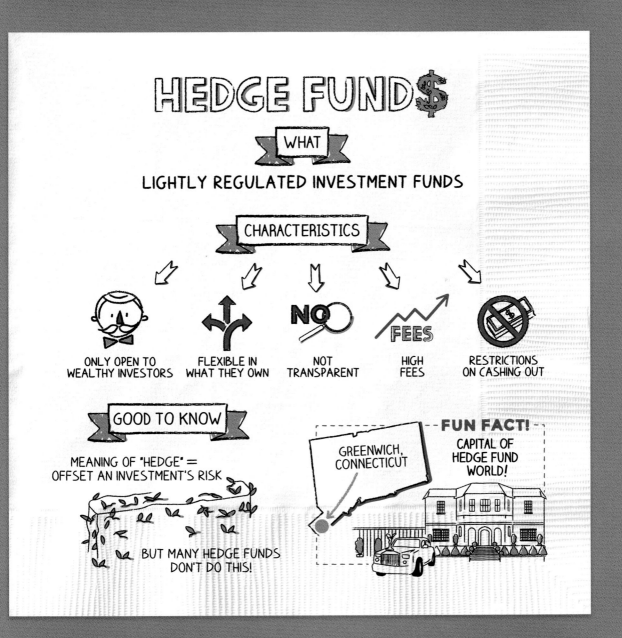

Types

The many flavors of hedge funds can include:

> Long-short—Bet that some stocks will go up and others will go down.
> Activist—Take big stakes in troubled companies and try to force changes to improve the stock value.
> Macro—Bet on big-picture global-economy issues, such as the likelihood that China will go into a recession, or that the U.S. dollar will fall.
> Distressed debt—Buy the debt of companies that are on the brink of failure at a big discount.
> Film—Some funds finance movies.
> Art—Some funds manage a basket of high-value fine art.

"A hedge fund is a fee structure in search of a strategy."

—UNKNOWN

Fun Facts

> The word *hedge* has a specific meaning in investing—it means to reduce risk by making an investment that offsets the risk of another investment. A common misconception is that hedge funds engage in hedging. Some do, but plenty don't.
> At one point in time, Bernie Madoff's hedge fund was thought to be the largest in the world.

> Just like Silicon Valley is the capital of the tech world, Greenwich, Connecticut, is the capital of the hedge fund world.

Key Takeaways

> Hedge funds are professionally managed funds that pool investors' money, like mutual funds.
> Unlike mutual funds, hedge funds generally charge high fees, offer limited disclosures to investors, and may restrict when investors can withdraw their money.
> Although hedge funds can follow many different types of investment strategies, they generally tend to be a high-risk investment option.

A *hedge fund* is a fancy name for an investment partnership, just like *finger pants* is a fancy name for gloves. —Napkin Finance ☺

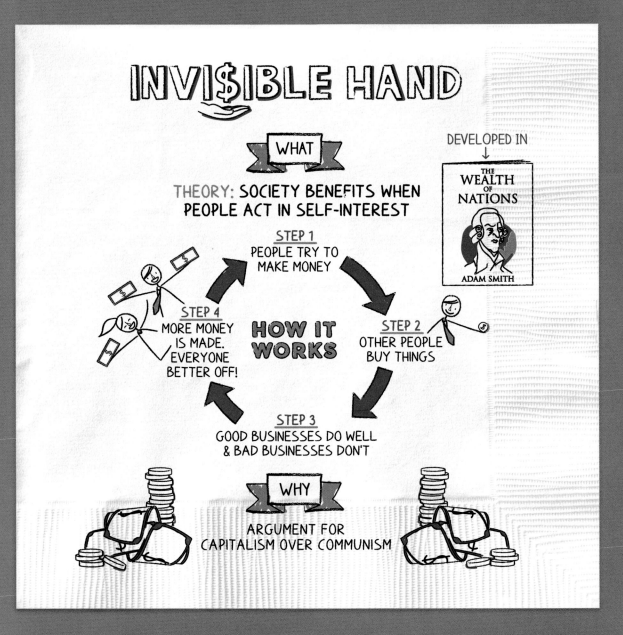

Invisible Hand

The "invisible hand" is an economic theory developed by Adam Smith. It proposes that when people act in their self-interest it unintentionally benefits society at large. In a capitalist economy, an invisible hand guides everyone's actions toward the one that will benefit society the most (or so the theory goes).

How It Works

The invisible hand theory argues that capitalism creates a virtuous circle:

Step 1: People try to make money. They start companies and sell goods and services.

Step 2: Other people decide for themselves how much to buy of certain things. If they buy more of something, companies produce more of that thing. If they buy less of something, companies produce less of that thing.

Step 3: Good businesses do well and bad businesses don't.

Step 4: More money is made, more money is spent, and more people have jobs. Everyone is better off.

> "It is not from the benevolence of the butcher, the brewer, or the baker that we expect our dinner, but from their regard to their own interest."
> —ADAM SMITH, ECONOMIST

Why Used

The invisible hand theory is generally used to argue in favor of capitalism—in which people are free to decide what job to have and how to spend their money—over communism—in which the government decides these things.

	Capitalism	Planned economy (aka communism)
What job do you have?	You're free to pick (and change your mind).	The government tells you what job to do.
What stuff can you buy?	Whatever you want, as long as you can afford it.	The government may ration goods, or distribute them on a predetermined basis.
Who decides what gets made?	Companies, or other producers, decide.	The government tells, say, shoemakers how many shoes to make in a given year.
Who bears the risk?	Individuals bear the risk. If you can't make money, you're poor. If you do well, you get rich.	Society bears the risk. No one gets rich or poor (in theory).

Fun Facts

> › It wasn't just the self-interest of the butcher and the baker that put Adam Smith's dinner on the table—his mother cooked his dinners until she died (when Smith was in his sixties).
> › To paraphrase Jeff Goldblum: Capitalism will find a way. Cigarettes, gold, and U.S. dollars have all served as alternate currencies in restricted

economies, such as communist nations and prisons. (Ramen noodles have overtaken cigarettes as the currency of choice in U.S. prisons.)

Key Takeaways

› The invisible hand theory argues that society and the economy are better off when people are allowed to decide for themselves how to make money and what to buy.

› It's generally used as an argument in favor of capitalism over communism, in which the government plans and decides what is produced and what jobs people have.

The last thing you want is the invisible hand of the marketplace giving you the finger. —Napkin Finance ☺

Game Theory

Game theory is an economic model for predicting people's decisions in tricky situations.

Example

The classic game theory example is called the prisoner's dilemma. In this hypothetical situation, two accomplices are arrested by the police. How much prison time they'll get depends on whether they confess or stay silent:

	Prisoner 1 confesses (and rats out Prisoner 2)	Prisoner 1 doesn't confess
Prisoner 2 confesses (and rats out Prisoner 1)	Both confess → Both get 5 years	Prisoner 2 confesses → Gets 0 years Prisoner 1 doesn't → Gets 8 years
Prisoner 2 doesn't confess	Prisoner 1 confesses → Gets 0 years Prisoner 2 doesn't → Gets 8 years	Neither confesses → Both get 6 months

Obviously, the best-case scenario is for neither to confess. But the cops are questioning Prisoner 1 and Prisoner 2 in separate rooms, and neither knows what the other will do.

From Prisoner 1's point of view, whether or not Prisoner 2 confesses, Prisoner 1 is better off by confessing (and ratting out Prisoner 2). If Prisoner 2 does confess (and rats outs Prisoner 1), Prisoner 1 cuts his prison time from eight years to five years by also confessing. If Prisoner 2 doesn't confess, Prisoner 1 can cut his prison time from half a year to zero by confessing (and ratting out Prisoner 2).

The same logic goes for Prisoner 2. The model predicts that in the end, they'll both end up ratting each other out. (This is called a Nash equilibrium—named for the economist John Nash, who developed the theory.)

How Used

In the real world, game theory can be used to model decisions in situations such as:

> Business negotiations.

> Corporate strategy.

> Gambling.

> Military tactics.

Fun Facts

> When some researchers tested out the prisoner's dilemma with real prisoners, the prisoners ratted each other out less than half the time— much less than the model predicts. (Granted, the payoff was coffee and cigarettes, not reduced sentences.)

> Game theory has been used to model outcomes in nuclear standoffs like the Cuban Missile Crisis. (Seems like it's worked so far, since we're still here.)

> In the movie *A Beautiful Mind,* John Nash has his revelation about game theory when he and all his friends want to talk to the same woman at a bar. He realizes if they all go for her then none of them will get her, so they ignore her and talk to her friends instead.

Key Takeaways

› Game theory is an approach to predicting people's decisions in strategic situations.
› The theory models behavior by looking at what one party will do, given that it can't predict or control what the other side will do.
› Game theory can be used to model business and military decision-making.

If you hold a chess piece to your ear, you can hear a thorough explanation of game theory. —Napkin Finance 😊

Chapter Quiz

1. The rule of 72 is:

   a. An investing rule of thumb that if you're not rich by age seventy-two, you never will be.
   b. A rule of thumb for determining how much of your money to hold in stocks.
   c. A way of estimating how long it will take your money to double, at a given return rate.
   d. Your weird friend's description of his dating age range.

2. Crowdfunding is:

   a. A way of earning a return by scamming lots of people out of very small amounts of money.
   b. A way of sourcing investment ideas from the Internet.
   c. When you steal people's wallets at concerts.
   d. A way to raise funds from lots of individual people through the power of the Internet.

3. **The key steps to launching a crowdfunding campaign include:**

   a. Choosing a crowdfunding website and writing your pitch.
   b. Filing a notice with the Federal Reserve.
   c. Wearing a zany suit with dollar signs all over it.
   d. Sending Venmo requests to your most successful friends from high school.

4. **Types of crowdfunding can include:**

   a. Equity-based, in which investors receive ownership in a venture.
   b. Loans, in which investors are paid back with interest.
   c. Rewards-based, in which investors may receive an early version of the product being developed.
   d. All of the above.

5. **True or false: One big advantage of investing in a crowdfunding campaign is that your investment is typically insured by the FDIC.**

   ○ True   ○ False

6. **The main reasons people tend to get involved in philanthropy include:**

   a. The chance to earn big profits.
   b. The tax breaks and the warm fuzzy feelings it gives them.
   c. Heaven-might-exist insurance.
   d. Not realizing what *philanthropy* means before it's too late.

7. **Ways to give back can include:**

   a. Tipping baristas.
   b. Using metal straws.
   c. Self-care.
   d. Impact investing.

8. **True or false: Donations to needy individuals' crowdfunding campaigns generally aren't tax-deductible.**

   ○ True   ○ False

9. **A hedge fund is:**

   a. A mutual fund that hedges its risks.
   b. A lightly regulated fund that typically charges high fees.
   c. Something your gardener's been trying to get you to invest in.
   d. What sleazy guys say they're managers of when they're actually unemployed con artists.

10. **Unlike a mutual fund, in which anyone may invest, to invest in a hedge fund you have to:**

    a. Meet a certain minimum level of assets or income.
    b. Pass a test about investing knowledge first.
    c. Play golf with the fund manager's brother-in-law.
    d. Be a member of Skull and Bones.

11. **True or false: Hedge funds are well regulated and there haven't been any major hedge-fund scandals or frauds.**

    ○ True   ○ False

12. **In a nutshell, the "invisible hand" is:**

    a. The excuse you give when your roommate asks who took all his beer.
    b. Another term for the FICA deductions from your paycheck.
    c. An economic theory used to argue in favor of capitalism over communism.
    d. A dirty term in Urban Dictionary.

13. **The defining characteristic of capitalism, as opposed to communism, is:**

    a. More Kardashians.
    b. Dance parties are legal, versus illegal.
    c. A centralized stock market, as opposed to a decentralized market.
    d. People decide for themselves how to try to earn a living and what to consume, instead of the government deciding.

14. **Game theory is:**

    a. An economic model for predicting strategic decisions.
    b. A trading strategy used by cryptocurrency investors.
    c. A Reddit forum about Fortnite.
    d. How Warren Buffett picks stocks.

15. **Game theory can be used in:**

    a. Corporate strategy.
    b. Military strategy.
    c. Pickup-artist strategy.
    d. All of the above.

Answers

1. c	**5.** f	**9.** b	**13.** d
2. d	**6.** b	**10.** a	**14.** a
3. a	**7.** d	**11.** f	**15.** d
4. d	**8.** t	**12.** c	

Conclusion

Congratulations, you've finished the book and now you're rich
(with knowledge)!

Hopefully, you're also feeling confident enough to put some
of your newfound skills to use: such as by checking in on your credit
score, taking a peek at your 401(k) balance, or finally funding that
emergency savings account.

Whether you go on to make billions after you put this book down or
you end up moving back in with your parents for the third time,
at least you're now better equipped to handle financial decisions.

If you're interested in seeing more napkins, you can visit us at
NapkinFinance.com

Money can't buy you happiness, but it's still better to cry in a
Bentley than on a bus. —Napkin Finance ☺

Acknowledgments

This book would not have been possible without the love and hard work of so many people. Thank you to everyone who has supported Napkin Finance from the beginning and sent us suggestions, notes, and ideas. Our community has provided the strength and passion that made this book possible and it continues to build the movement to empower millions of people.

First of all, I am grateful to the entire Napkin Finance team. A big thank-you goes to Elizabeth Leary, whose brilliant words helped make Napkin Finance not only fun to read but also educational, engaging, and accurate. She is our MVP—a superstar who is incredibly talented and graceful under pressure. There are few people who can write about finance and also make it funny and relatable. Elizabeth—I am forever grateful to have you by my side on the Napkin Finance journey. Thank you to the remarkable Gregg Friedman, for making the visuals and napkins come together. We are lucky to have had your guidance and magic touch in creating beautiful images from cover to cover. Thank you to Wirdy, our secret weapon, who has a gift for making illustrations pop and can tell a story in a way that is always unique and fun. Eden Dranger and Alejandro Bien-Willner— thank you for your comedic brilliance and special touch.

This book would never have happened without the backing of Byrd Leavell at UTA, who always believed a Napkin Finance book was a good idea. Thank you to the entire

Dey Street and HarperCollins team—our amazing editor, Matthew Daddona, and Julie Paulauski and Kendra Newton, for your hard work and tireless efforts.

Thank you to the faculty and staff at Harvard Business School, and my favorite finance professor, Mihir Desai, whose class provided the first spark of inspiration that led to Napkin Finance.

Most of all, I want to thank my family. My parents, Mehrzad and John Hay, for their unconditional love. They have supported every crazy idea and dream I have had over the years. I am truly the luckiest person to have you in my life. My amazing, kind-hearted, and brilliant sister, Atoosa; my brother-in-law, Alex; and my three loves, Lauren, Jonathan, and Julia Nehorai, who inspire me in a million ways. And to my remarkable brother, David, whom I love and look up to more than he will ever know.

Bibliography

Chapter 1: Money 101

Anderson, Joel. "Survey Finds Most Common Reasons Americans Use Emergency Funds." *GO Banking Rates,* May 24, 2018. https://www.gobankingrates.com/saving-money/budgeting/how-americans-use-emergency-fund.

Armstrong, Martin A. "Part I of IV—A Brief History of World Credit & Interest Rates." Armstrong Economics. Accessed March 2, 2019. https://www.armstrongeconomics.com/research/a-brief-history-of-world-credit-interest-rates/3000-b-c-500-a-d-the-ancient-economy.

BankRate. "Credit Card Minimum Payment Calculator." Accessed March 2, 2019. https://www.bankrate.com/calculators/credit-cards/credit-card-minimum-payment.aspx.

Bawden-Davis, Julie. "10 Powerful Quotes from Warren Buffett That'll Change Your Perception About Money and Success." SuperMoney. Updated June 2, 2017. https://www.supermoney.com/2014/04/10-powerful-personal-finance-quotes-from-warren-buffett.

Bella, Rick. "Clackamas Bank Robber Demands $1, Waits for Police to Take Him to Jail." *Oregon Live.* Updated January 2019. Posted in 2014. https://www.oregonlive.com/clackamascounty/2013/08/clackamas_bank_robber_demands.html.

Board of Governors of the Federal Reserve System. "Consumer Credit-G.19." February 7, 2019. https://www.federalreserve.gov/releases/g19/current/#fn3a.

Board of Governors of the Federal Reserve System. "Report on the Economic Well-Being of U.S. Households in 2017." Published May 2018. https://www.federalreserve.gov/publications/files/2017-report-economic-well-being-us-households-201805.pdf.

Bureau of Labor Statistics. "Consumer Expenditure Surveys." Last modified September 11, 2018. https://www.bls.gov/cex/tables.htm#annual.

El Issa, Erin. "How to Combat Emotional Spending." *U.S. News & World Report,* February 28, 2017. https://money.usnews.com/money/blogs/my-money/articles/2017-02-28/how-to-combat-emotional-overspending.

Forbes. "Thoughts On the Business of Life." Accessed March 2, 2019. https://www.forbes.com/quotes/1274.

Freedman, Anne. "Top Five Uninsurable Risks." *Risk & Insurance,* September 2, 2014. https://riskandinsurance.com/top-five-uninsurable-risks.

Huddleston, Cameron. "58% of Americans Have Less Than $1,000 in Savings." *GO Banking Rates,* December 21, 2018. https://www.gobankingrates.com/saving-money/savings -advice/average-american-savings-account-balance.

Jellett, Deborah. "The 10 Strangest Things Ever Insured." *The Richest,* May 10, 2014. https:// www.therichest.com/rich-list/the-most-shocking-and-bizarre-things-ever-insured-2.

Jézégou, Frédérick. "If You Think Nobody Cares If You're Alive, Try Missing a Couple of Car Payments." *Dictionary of Quotes,* November 23, 2008. https://www.dictionary -quotes.com/if-you-think-nobody-cares-if-you-re-alive-try-missing-a-couple-of-car -payments-flip-wilson.

Marks, Gene. "This Bank Will Take Cheese as Collateral." *Washington Post,* April 17, 2017. https://www.washingtonpost.com/news/on-small-business/wp/2017/04/17/this-bank -will-take-cheese-as-collateral/?noredirect=on&utm_term=.928e4f2fdff7.

Merriman, Paul A. "The Genius of Warren Buffett in 23 Quotes." *MarketWatch,* August 19, 2015. https://www.marketwatch.com/story/the-genius-of-warren-buffett-in-23 -quotes-2015-08-19.

Mortgage Professor. "What Is Predatory Lending?" Updated July 18, 2007. https:// mtgprofessor.com/A%20-%20Predatory%20Lending/what_is_predatory_lending.htm.

Peterson, Bailey. "Credit Card Spending Studies (2018 Report): Why You Spend More When You Pay With a Credit Card." ValuePenguin. Accessed March 2, 2019. https://www .valuepenguin.com/credit-cards/credit-card-spending-studies.

Pierce, Tony. "$1 Bank Robbery Doesn't Pay Off for Man Who Said He Was Desperate for Healthcare." *Los Angeles Times,* June 21, 2011. https://latimesblogs.latimes.com /washington/2011/06/1-bank-robbery-doesnt-pay-off-for-healthcare-hopeful.html.

Randow, Jana and Kennedy, Simon. "Negative Interest Rates." *Bloomberg,* March 21, 2017. https://www.bloomberg.com/quicktake/negative-interest-rates.

Tsosie, Claire and El Issa, Erin. "2018 American Household Credit Card Debt Study." NerdWallet, December 10, 2018. https://www.nerdwallet.com/blog/average-credit-card -debt-household.

Tuttle, Brad. "Cheapskate Wisdom from . . . Benjamin Franklin." *Time,* September 23, 2009. http://business.time.com/2009/09/23/cheapskate-wisdom-from-benjamin-franklin-2.

Chapter 2: Credit Where It's Due

Carrns, Ann. "New Type of Credit Score Aims to Widen Pool of Borrowers." *New York Times,* October 26, 2018. https://www.nytimes.com/2018/10/26/your-money/new-credit -score-fico.html.

Credit Karma. "How Many Credit Scores Do I Have?" May 14, 2016. https://www.creditkarma
.com/advice/i/how-many-credit-scores-do-i-have.

CreditScoreDating.com. "CreditScoreDating.com: Where Good Credit is Sexy." Accessed
March 2, 2019. www.creditscoredating.com.

Dictionary.com. "Credit." Accessed March 2, 2019. https://www.dictionary.com/browse
/credit.

Eveleth, Rose. "Forty Years Ago, Women Had a Hard Time Getting Credit Cards."
Smithsonian.com, January 8, 2014. https://www.smithsonianmag.com/smart-news
/forty-years-ago-women-had-a-hard-time-getting-credit-cards-180949289.

Fair Isaac Corporation. "5 Factors that Determine a FICO® Score." September 23, 2016.
https://blog.myfico.com/5-factors-determine-fico-score.

Fair Isaac Corporation. "Average U.S. Fico Score Hits New High." September 24, 2018.
https://www.fico.com/blogs/risk-compliance/average-u-s-fico-score-hits-new-high.

Garfinkel, Simpson. "Separating Equifax from Fiction." *Wired,* September 1, 1995. https://
www.wired.com/1995/09/equifax.

Gonzalez-Garcia, Jamie. "Credit Card Ownership Statistics." CreditCards.com. Updated
April 26, 2018. https://www.creditcards.com/credit-card-news/ownership-statistics.php.

Guy-Birken, Emily. "8 Fun Facts About Credit Cards." WiseBread. May 24, 2018. https://www
.wisebread.com/8-fun-facts-about-credit-cards.

Herron, Janna. "How FICO Became 'The' Credit Score." *BankRate,* December 12, 2013.
https://finance.yahoo.com/news/fico-became-credit-score-100000037.html.

Rotter, Kimberly. "A History of the Three Credit Bureaus." CreditRepair.com. Accessed
March 2, 2019. https://www.creditrepair.com/blog/credit-score/credit-bureau-history.

United States Census Bureau. "U.S. and World Population Clock." Accessed March 3, 2019.
https://www.census.gov/popclock.

Chapter 3: Buy Low, Sell High

Ajayi, Akin. "The Rise of the Robo-Advisers." Credit Suisse, July 15, 2015. https://www
.credit-suisse.com/corporate/en/articles/news-and-expertise/the-rise-of-the-robo
-advisers-201507.html.

Allocca, Sean. "Goldman Sachs Comes to Main Street with 'Broader' Wealth Offering."
Financial Planning, October 22, 2018. https://www.financial-planning.com/news
/goldman-sachs-marcus-robo-advisor-merge-wealth-management.

American Oil & Gas Historical Society. "Cities Service Company." Accessed March 2, 2019.
https://aoghs.org/stocks/cities-service-company.

Anderson, Nathan. "15 Weird Hedge Fund Strategies That Investors Should Know About." ClaritySpring. August 24, 2015. http://www.clarityspring.com/15-weird-hedge-fund -strategies.

Bakke, David. "The Top 17 Investing Quotes of All Time." Investopedia. Updated November 30, 2016. https://www.investopedia.com/financial-edge/0511/the-top-17-investing -quotes-of-all-time.aspx.

Collinson, Patrick. "The Truth About Investing: Women Do It Better than Men." *Guardian,* November 24, 2018. https://www.theguardian.com/money/2018/nov/24/the-truth -about-investing-women-do-it-better-than-men.

Damodaran, Aswath. "Annual Returns on Stock, T. Bonds and T. Bills: 1928-Current." NYU Stern School of Business. Updated January 5, 2019. http://pages.stern.nyu .edu/~adamodar/New_Home_Page/datafile/histretSP.html.

Deloitte. "The Expansion of Robo-Advisory in Wealth Management." August 2016. https:// www2.deloitte.com/content/dam/Deloitte/de/Documents/financial-services/Deloitte -Robo-safe.pdf.

De Sousa, Agnieszka and Kumar, Nishant. "Citadel Hires Cumulus Energy Traders; Hedge Fund Shuts." *Bloomberg,* April 27, 2018. https://www.bloomberg.com/news /articles/2018-04-27/citadel-hires-cumulus-founder-and-fund-s-traders-in-energy -push.

Elkins, Kathleen. "Warren Buffett Is 88 Today—Here's What He Learned from Buying His First Stock at Age 11." CNBC, August 30, 2018. https://www.cnbc.com/2018/08/30/when -warren-buffett-bought-his-first-stock-and-what-he-learned.html.

Eule, Alex. "As Robo-Advisors Cross $200 Billion in Assets, Schwab Leads in Performance." *Barron's,* February 3, 2018. https://www.barrons.com/articles/as-robo-advisors-cross -200-billion-in-assets-schwab-leads-in-performance-1517509393.

Fidelity Investments. "Who's the Better Investor: Men or Women?" May 18, 2017. https:// www.fidelity.com/about-fidelity/individual-investing/better-investor-men-or-women.

Hamilton, Walter. "Madoff's Returns Aroused Doubts." *Los Angeles Times,* December 13, 2008. http://articles.latimes.com/2008/dec/13/business/fi-madoff13.

Hiller, David, Draper, Paul, and Faff, Robert. "Do Precious Metals Shine? An Investment Perspective." CFA Institute, March/April 2006. https://www.cfapubs.org/doi/pdf/10.2469 /faj.v62.n2.4085.

Loomis, Carol J. "The Inside Story of Warren Buffett." *Fortune,* April 11, 1988. http://fortune .com/1988/04/11/warren-buffett-inside-story.

Merriman, Paul A. "The Genius of John Bogle in 9 Quotes." *MarketWatch,* November

25, 2016. https://www.marketwatch.com/story/the-genius-of-john-bogle-in-9-quotes-2016-11-23.

Ross, Sean. "Has Real Estate or the Stock Market Performed Better Historically?" *Investopedia*. Updated February 5, 2019. https://www.investopedia.com/ask /answers/052015/which-has-performed-better-historically-stock-market-or-real-estate .asp.

Shoot, Brittany. "Banksy 'Girl with Balloon' Painting Worth Double After Self-Destructing at Auction." *Fortune,* October 8, 2018. http://fortune.com/2018/10/08/banksy-girl-with -balloon-self-destructed-video-art-worth-double.

Siegel, Rene Shimada. "What I Would—and Did—Say to New Grads." *Inc.,* June 19, 2013. https://www.inc.com/rene-siegel/what-i-would-and-did-say-to-new-grads.html.

Udland, Myles. "Buffett: Volatility Is Not the Same Thing as Risk, and Investors Who Think It Is Will Cost Themselves Money." *Business Insider,* April 6, 2015. https://www .businessinsider.com/warren-buffett-on-risk-and-volatility-2015-4.

Walsgard, Jonas Cho. "Betting on Death Is Turning Out Better Than Expected for Hedge Fund." *Bloomberg,* February 11, 2019. https://www.bloomberg.com/news /articles/2019-02-11/betting-on-death-is-turning-better-than-expected-for-hedge -fund.

Chapter 4: Paying Your Dues

Bakke, David. "The Top 17 Investing Quotes of All Time." Investopedia. Updated November 30, 2016. https://www.investopedia.com/financial-edge/0511/the-top-17-investing -quotes-of-all-time.aspx.

Bloom, Ester. "4 Celebrities Who Didn't Pay off Their Student Loans Until Their 40s." CNBC, May 12, 2017. https://www.cnbc.com/2017/05/12/4-celebrities-who-didnt-pay-off -their-student-loans-until-their-40s.html.

The College Board. "Average Estimated Undergraduate Budgets 2018–19." Accessed March 2, 2019. https://trends.collegeboard.org/college-pricing/figures-tables/average -estimated-undergraduate-budgets-2018-19.

The College Board. "Average Rates of Growth of Published Charges by Decade." Accessed March 2, 2019. https://trends.collegeboard.org/college-pricing/figures-tables/average -rates-growth-published-charges-decade.

The College Board. "Trends in College Pricing 2017." Accessed March 2, 2019. https://trends .collegeboard.org/sites/default/files/2017-trends-in-college-pricing_0.pdf.

CollegeXpress. "60 of the Weirdest College Scholarships." Carnegie Dartlet. Updated May

2017. https://www.collegexpress.com/lists/list/60-of-the-weirdest-college
-scholarships/1000.

Federal Reserve Bank of St. Louis. "Student Loans Owned and Securitized, Outstanding."
Updated February 7, 2019. https://fred.stlouisfed.org/series/SLOAS.

Iuliano, Jason. "An Empirical Assessment of Student Loan Discharges and the Undue
Hardship Standard." *86 American Bankruptcy Law Journal 495* (2012). Available at SSRN:
https://papers.ssrn.com/sol3/papers.cfm?abstract_id=1894445.

Martis, Lily. "Best Entry-Level Jobs for College Grads." Monster. Accessed March 2, 2019.
https://www.monster.com/career-advice/article/best-entry-level-jobs.

Safier, Rebecca. "Survey: Majority of Student Loan Borrowers Don't Know How Interest or
Forgiveness Works." Student Loan Hero. Updated May 15, 2018. https://studentloanhero
.com/featured/survey-majority-student-loan-borrowers-know-interest-forgiveness
-works.

Sallie Mae. "How America Pays for College 2018." Accessed March 2, 2019. https://www
.salliemae.com/assets/research/HAP/HAP18_Infographic.pdf.

Sunstein, Cass R. "Making Government Logical." *New York Times,* September 19, 2015.
https://www.nytimes.com/2015/09/20/opinion/sunday/cass-sunstein-making
-government-logicalhtml.html.

T. Rowe Price. "Parents of Only Boys Place Greater Priority on College Than Parents of Only
Girls." September 21, 2017. https://www.prnewswire.com/news-releases/t-rowe
-price-parents-of-only-boys-place-greater-priority-on-college-than-parents-of-only
-girls-300523653.html.

U.S. Army. "Using the GI Bill." Updated November 6, 2018. https://www.goarmy.com
/benefits/education-benefits/using-the-gi-bill.html.

U.S. Department of Education. "Avoid Scams While Searching for Scholarships, Filling Out
the FAFSA® Form, Repaying Your Student Loans, or Giving Personal Information to
Schools and Lenders." Accessed March 2, 2019. https://studentaid.ed.gov/sa/types
/scams#dont-pay-for-fafsa.

U.S. Department of Education. "iLibrary—Federal School Code List." Accessed March 2, 2019.
https://ifap.ed.gov/ifap/fedSchoolCodeList.jsp.

U.S. Department of Education. "Types of Aid." Accessed March 2, 2019. https://studentaid
.ed.gov/sa/types.

U.S. Inflation Calculator. "Historical Inflation Rates: 1914–2019." Coinnews Media Group LLC.
Updated February 13, 2019. https://www.usinflationcalculator.com/inflation
/historical-inflation-rates.

The Vanguard Group. "What's the Average Cost of College?" The Vanguard Group. Accessed March 2, 2019. https://investor.vanguard.com/college-savings-plans/average-cost-of-college.

The World Bank Group. "GDP (current US$)." Accessed March 2, 2019. https://data.worldbank.org/indicator/NY.GDP.MKTP.CD?year_high_desc=true.

Chapter 5: Into the Sunset

"A Growing Cult of Millennials Is Obsessed With Early Retirement. This 72-Year-Old is their Unlikely Inspiration." *Money,* April 17, 2018. http://money.com/money/5241566/vicki-robin-financial-independence-retire-early.

Anderson, Robert. "Retirement No Longer Compulsory for Emiratis after 25 Years of Service." *Gulf Business,* June 6, 2018. https://gulfbusiness.com/retirement-no-longer-compulsory-for-emiratis-after-25-years.

Aperion Care. "Retirement Age Around the Globe." Accessed March 2, 2019. https://aperioncare.com/blog/retirement-age-around-world.

Berger, Rob. "Top 100 Money Quotes of All Time." *Forbes,* April 30, 2014. https://www.forbes.com/sites/robertberger/2014/04/30/top-100-money-quotes-of-all-time/#7ae183444998.

"Do the Dutch Have the Pension Problem Solved?" *PBS NewsHour,* November 10, 2013. https://www.pbs.org/newshour/show/do-the-dutch-have-the-pension-problem-solved.

Fidelity Investments. "Fidelity Q3 Retirement Analysis: Account Balances Hit Record Highs 10 Years Following Financial Crisis." November 5, 2018. https://www.fidelity.com/bin-public/060_www_fidelity_com/documents/press-release/fidelity-q3-2018-account-balances-hit-record-highs.pdf.

Hylton, J. Gordon. "The Devil's Disciple and the Learned Profession: Ambrose Bierce and the Practice of Law in Gilded Age America." Marquette University Law School. January 1, 1991. https://scholarship.law.marquette.edu/cgi/viewcontent.cgi?referer=https://www.google.com/&httpsredir=1&article=1474&context=facpub.

Mauldin, John. "Someone Is Spending Your Pension Money." *Forbes,* October 26, 2015. https://www.forbes.com/sites/johnmauldin/2015/10/26/someone-is-spending-your-pension-money/#36069e677fd0.

Morgan, Richard. "Jimi Hendrix's Family Can't Stop Suing Each Other." *New York Post,* March 24, 2017. https://nypost.com/2017/03/24/jimi-hendrixs-family-cant-stop-suing-each-other-over-estate.

Social Security Administration. "What Prisoners Need to Know." Accessed March 2, 2019. https://www.ssa.gov/pubs/EN-05-10133.pdf.

Chapter 6: A Wild Ride

Amadeo, Kimberly. "Wall Street: How It Works, Its History, and Its Crashes." The Balance. Updated January 21, 2019. https://www.thebalance.com/wall-street-how-it-works-history-and-crashes-3306252.

Bowden, Ebony. "History's Biggest 'Fat-Finger' Trading Errors." *The New Daily,* October 2, 2014. https://thenewdaily.com.au/money/finance-news/2014/10/02/historys-biggest-fat-finger-trading-errors.

Chen, James. "Bowie Bond." Investopedia. Updated March 7, 2018. https://www.investopedia.com/terms/b/bowie-bond.asp.

Clark, Andrew. "The Man Who Blew the Whistle on Bernard Madoff." *Guardian,* March 24, 2010. https://www.theguardian.com/business/2010/mar/24/bernard-madoff-whistleblower-harry-markopolos.

Cohn, Laura. "Boost Your IQ with a Good Book." *Kiplinger's Personal Finance,* November 2009.

Crestmont Research. "Returns over 20-Year Periods Vary Significantly; Affected by the Starting P/E Ratio." Accessed March 2, 2019. https://www.crestmontresearch.com/docs/Stock-20-Yr-Returns.pdf.

"Dow Jones Industrial Average All-Time Largest One Day Gains and Losses." *Wall Street Journal.* Accessed March 2, 2019. http://www.wsj.com/mdc/public/page/2_3024-djia_alltime.html.

Encyclopædia Britannica. "Wall Street." Accessed March 2, 2019. https://www.britannica.com/topic/Wall-Street-New-York-City.

Epstein, Gene. "Prepare for Lower Stock Returns." *Barron's.* Updated January 23, 2018. https://www.barrons.com/articles/prepare-for-lower-stock-returns-1516666766.

Faulkenberry, Ken. "Value Investing Quotes, Sayings, & Proverbs: Wisest Men Compilation." Arbor Investment Planner. Accessed March 2, 2019. http://www.arborinvestmentplanner.com/wisest-value-investing-quotes-sayings-money-proverbs.

First Trust Portfolios L.P. "History of U.S. Bear & Bull Markets Since 1926." Accessed March 2, 2019. https://www.ftportfolios.com/Common/ContentFileLoader.aspx?ContentGUID=4ecfa978-d0bb-4924-92c8-628ff9bfe12d.

Investment Company Institute. "ETF Assets and Net Issuance January 2019." February 27, 2019. https://www.ici.org/research/stats/etf/etfs_01_19.

Kirchheimer, Sid. "10 Fun Facts About Money." AARP. Accessed March 2, 2019. https://www
.aarp.org/money/investing/info-03-2012/money-facts.html.

Landis, David. "ETFs That Miss the Mark." *Kiplinger,* July 31, 2007. https://www.kiplinger
.com/article/investing/T022-C000-S002-etfs-that-miss-the-mark.html.

Mahmudova, Anora. "Investors Can Bet on Whether People Will Get Fit, Fat, or Old with
These ETFs." *MarketWatch,* June 18, 2016. https://www.marketwatch.com/story/new
-obesity-and-fitness-etfs-follow-demographic-trends-2016-06-09.

MFS. "Over 90 and Still Active." Accessed March 2, 2019. https://www.mfs.com/who-we
-are/our-history.html.

Phung, Albert. "Why Do Companies Issue 100-Year Bonds?" Investopedia. Updated July 2,
2018. https://www.investopedia.com/ask/answers/06/100yearbond.asp.

"The World's Largest Hedge Fund Is a Fraud." Securities Exchange Commission, submission
on November 7, 2005. https://www.sec.gov/news/studies/2009/oig-509/exhibit-0293
.pdf.

Waxman, Olivia B. "How a Financial Panic Helped Launch the New York Stock Exchange."
Time, May 17, 2017. http://time.com/4777959/buttonwood-agreement-stock-exchange.

World Gold Council. "FAQs." Accessed March 2, 2019. http://www.spdrgoldshares.com
/usa/faqs.

World Gold Council. "Gold Bar List and Inspectorate Certificates." Accessed March 2, 2019.
http://www.spdrgoldshares.com/usa/gold-bar-list.

Yahoo! Finance. "Amazon.com, Inc. (AMZN)." Accessed March 1, 2019. https://finance
.yahoo.com/quote/AMZN/key-statistics?p=AMZN.

Chapter 7: EZ Does It

Beck, Emma. "Cutting That Bagel Will Cost You: Weird State Tax Laws." *USA Today,* March 31,
2013. https://www.usatoday.com/story/money/personalfinance/2013/03/31/odd-state
-tax-laws/1951911.

Dodds, Colin. "Dr. Dre: Most Influential Quotes." Investopedia. Accessed March 2, 2019.
https://www.investopedia.com/university/dr-dre-biography/dr-dre-most-influential
-quotes.asp.

eFile.com. "Unusual but Legitimate Tax Breaks." Accessed March 2, 2019. https://www.efile
.com/legitimate-tax-breaks-and-unusual-extraordinary-qualified-tax-deductions-and
-tax-exemptions.

Internal Revenue Service. "Tax Quotes." Page last reviewed or updated August 21, 2018.
https://www.irs.gov/newsroom/tax-quotes.

Intuit. "10 Strange but Legitimate Federal Tax Deductions." Intuit Turbotax, updated for Tax Year 2017. Accessed March 2, 2019. https://turbotax.intuit.com/tax-tips/tax-deductions-and-credits/10-strange-but-legitimate-federal-tax-deductions/L6A6QzGiV.

Intuit. "11 Strange State Tax Laws." Intuit Turbotax, updated for Tax Year 2018. Accessed March 2, 2019. https://turbotax.intuit.com/tax-tips/fun-facts/12-strange-state-tax-laws/L4qENY2nZ.

James, Geoffrey. "130 Inspirational Quotes About Taxes." *Inc.,* April 13, 2015. https://www.inc.com/geoffrey-james/130-inspirational-quotes-about-taxes.html.

Leary, Elizabeth. "Special-Needs Families May Get Squeezed by Tax Reform." CNBC, November 9, 2017. https://www.cnbc.com/2017/11/09/special-needs-families-may-get-squeezed-by-tax-reform.html.

Sifferlin, Alexandra. "Tax Day Hazard: Fatal Crashes Increase on April 15." *Time,* April 11, 2012. http://healthland.time.com/2012/04/11/tax-day-hazard-fatal-crashes-increase-on-deadline-day.

Tax Policy Center. "How Could We Improve the Federal Tax System?" Accessed March 2, 2019. https://www.taxpolicycenter.org/briefing-book/what-other-countries-use-return-free-tax-filing.

Welsh, Monica. "Student Loan Interest Deduction." H&R Block, February 20, 2018. https://www.hrblock.com/tax-center/filing/adjustments-and-deductions/student-loan-deduction.

Wood, Robert W. "Defining Employees and Independent Contractors." *Business Law Today* Volume 17, Number 5, American Bar Association, May/June 2008. https://apps.americanbar.org/buslaw/blt/2008-05-06/wood.shtml.

Chapter 8: Go Big

Del Rey, Jason. "The Rise of Giant Consumer Startups That Said No to Investor Money." *Recode,* August 29, 2018. https://www.recode.net/2018/8/29/17774878/consumer-startups-business-model-native-mvmt-tuft-needle.

Desjardins, Jeff. "These 5 Companies All Started in a Garage, and Are Now Worth Billions of Dollars Apiece." *Business Insider,* June 29, 2016. https://www.businessinsider.com/billion-dollar-companies-started-in-garage-2016-6.

Economy, Peter. "17 Powerfully Inspiring Quotes from Southwest Airlines Founder Herb Kelleher." *Inc.,* January 4, 2019. https://www.inc.com/peter-economy/17-powerfully-inspiring-quotes-from-southwest-airlines-founder-herb-kelleher.html.

Farr, Christina. "Inside Silicon Valley's Culture of Spin." *Fast Company,* May 16, 2016. https://www.fastcompany.com/3059761/inside-silicon-valleys-culture-of-spin.

Gaskins, Tony A., Jr. *The Dream Chaser: If You Don't Build Your Dream, Someone Will Hire You to Build Theirs.* New Jersey: Wiley, 2016.

Guinness Book of World Records. "Most Patents Credited as Inventor." Accessed March 2, 2019. http://www.guinnessworldrecords.com/world-records/most-patents-held-by-a-person.

Hendricks, Drew. "6 $25 Billion Companies That Started in a Garage." *Inc.,* July 24, 2014. https://www.inc.com/drew-hendricks/6-25-billion-companies-that-started-in-a-garage.html.

Huet, Ellen. "Silicon Valley's $400 Juicer May Be Feeling the Squeeze." *Bloomberg,* April 19, 2017. https://www.bloomberg.com/news/features/2017-04-19/silicon-valley-s-400-juicer-may-be-feeling-the-squeeze.

Walker, Tim. "The Big Ideas That Started on a Napkin—From Reaganomics to Shark Week." *Guardian,* April 10, 2017. https://www.theguardian.com/us-news/shortcuts/2017/apr/10/napkin-ideas-mri-reaganomics-shark-week.

Zipkin, Nina. "20 Facts About the World's Billion-Dollar Startups." *Entrepreneur,* January 27, 2017. https://www.entrepreneur.com/article/288420.

Chapter 9: Voodoo Economics

"The Big Mac Index." *The Economist,* January 10, 2019. https://www.economist.com/news/2019/01/10/the-big-mac-index.

Corcoran, Kieran. "California's Economy Is Now the 5th-Biggest in the World, and Has Overtaken the United Kingdom." *Business Insider,* May 5, 2018. https://www.businessinsider.com/california-economy-ranks-5th-in-the-world-beating-the-uk-2018-5.

Davis, Marc. "How September 11 Affected the U.S. Stock Market." Investopedia, September 11, 2017. https://www.investopedia.com/financial-edge/0911/how-september-11-affected-the-u.s.-stock-market.aspx.

Kaifosh, Fred. "Why the Consumer Price Index Is Controversial." Investopedia. Updated October 12, 2018. https://www.investopedia.com/articles/07/consumerpriceindex.asp.

Lazette, Michelle Park. "The Crisis, the Fallout, the Change: The Great Recession in Retrospect." Federal Reserve Bank of Cleveland, December 18, 2017. https://www.clevelandfed.org/newsroom-and-events/multimedia-storytelling/recession-retrospective.aspx.

National Association of Theatre Owners. "Annual Average U.S. Ticket Price." Accessed March 2, 2019. http://www.natoonline.org/data/ticket-price.

National Bureau of Economic Research. "US Business Cycle Expansions and Contractions." Accessed March 2, 2019. https://www.nber.org/cycles.html.

Taylor, Andrea Browne. "How Much Did Things Cost in the 1980s?" *Kiplinger,* April 25, 2018. https://www.kiplinger.com/slideshow/spending/T050-S001-how-much-did-things-cost-in-the-1980s/index.html.

Wheelock, David C. "The Great Depression: An Overview." The Federal Reserve Bank of St. Louis. Accessed March 2, 2019. https://www.stlouisfed.org/~/media/files/pdfs/great-depression/the-great-depression-wheelock-overview.pdf.

Wolla, Scott A. "What's in Your Market Basket? Why Your Inflation Rate Might Differ from the Average." Federal Reserve Bank of St. Louis, October 2015. https://research.stlouisfed.org/publications/page1-econ/2015/10/01/whats-in-your-market-basket-why-your-inflation-rate-might-differ-from-the-average.

The World Bank. "Gross Domestic Product." January 25, 2019. https://databank.worldbank.org/data/download/GDP.pdf.

Chapter 10: The Bottom Line

Freifeld, Karen. "Kozlowski's $6,000 Shower Curtain to Find New Home." *Reuters,* June 14, 2012. https://www.reuters.com/article/us-tyco-curtain-idUSBRE85D1M620120614.

Kenton, Will. "What Is Worldcom?" Investopedia. Updated February 7, 2019. https://www.investopedia.com/terms/w/worldcom.asp.

Krugman, Paul. "Sam, Janet, and Fiscal Policy." *New York Times,* October 25, 2017. https://krugman.blogs.nytimes.com/2010/10/25/sam-janet-and-fiscal-policy.

Sage, Alexandria and Rai, Sonam. "Tesla CFO Leaves as Automaker Promises Profits and Cheaper Cars." *Reuters,* January 30, 2019. http://fortune.com/2017/02/27/oscars-2017-pricewaterhousecoopers -la-la-land.

Shen, Lucinda. "Why PwC Was Involved in the 2017 Oscars Best Picture Mix-Up." *Fortune,* February 27, 2017. http://fortune.com/2017/02/27/oscars-2017-pricewaterhousecoopers -la-la-land.

The Phrase Finder. "The Meaning and Origin of the Expression: Cooking the Books." Accessed March 2, 2019. https://www.phrases.org.uk/meanings/cook-the-books.html.

Thomas, C. William. "The Rise and Fall of Enron." *Journal of Accountancy,* April 1, 2002. https://www.journalofaccountancy.com/issues/2002/apr/theriseandfallofenron.html.

Yahoo! Finance. "Tesla, Inc. (TSLA)." Accessed March 1, 2019. https://finance.yahoo.com
/quote/TSLA/key-statistics?p=TSLA&.tsrc=fin-tre-srch.

Chapter 11: The Future of Money

"7 Major Companies That Accept Cryptocurrency." Due.com, January 31, 2018. https://www
.nasdaq.com/article/7-major-companies-that-accept-cryptocurrency-cm913745.

Blinder, Marc. "Making Cryptocurrency More Environmentally Sustainable." *Harvard Business Review,* November 27, 2018. https://hbr.org/2018/11/making-cryptocurrency-more
-environmentally-sustainable.

Browne, Ryan. "Burger King Has Launched Its Own Cryptocurrency in Russia Called 'WhopperCoin.'" CNBC, August 28, 2017. https://www.cnbc.com/2017/08/28/burger
-king-russia-cryptocurrency-whoppercoin.html.

Burchardi, Kaj and Harle, Nicolas. "The Blockchain Will Disrupt the Music Business and Beyond." *Wired,* January 20, 2018. https://www.wired.co.uk/article/blockchain-disrupting
-music-mycelia.

CoinMarketCap. "All Cryptocurrencies." Accessed March 2, 2019. https://coinmarketcap.com
/all/views/all.

Crane, Joy. "How Bitcoin Got Here: A (Mostly) Complete Timeline of Bitcoin's Highs and Lows." *New York,* December 28, 2017. http://nymag.com/intelligencer/2017/12/bitcoin
-timeline-bitcoins-record-highs-lows-and-history.html.

Cummins, Eleanor. "Cryptocurrency Millionaires Are Pushing Up Prices on Some Art and Collectibles." *Popular Science,* March 6, 2018. https://www.popsci.com/crypto-bitcoin
-millionaires-collectibles.

Cuthbertson, Anthony. "Man Accidentally Threw Bitcoin Worth $108 Million in the Trash, Says There's 'No Point Crying About It.'" *Newsweek,* November 30, 2017. https://www
.newsweek.com/man-accidentally-threw-bitcoin-worth-108m-trash-says-theres-no
-point-crying-726807.

Higgins, Stan. "The ICO Boxing Champ Floyd Mayweather Promoted Has Raised $30 Million Already." CoinDesk. Updated August 4, 2017. https://www.coindesk.com/ico-boxing
-champ-floyd-mayweather-promoted-raised-30-million-already.

Hinchcliffe, Emma. "10,000 Bitcoin Bought 2 Pizzas in 2010—And Now It'd Be Worth $20 Million." *Mashable,* May 23, 2017. https://mashable.com/2017/05/23/bitcoin-pizza-day
-20-million/#bMB2eoJdBmqs.

Marr, Bernard. "23 Fascinating Bitcoin and Blockchain Quotes Everyone Should Read." *Forbes,* August 15, 2018. https://www.forbes.com/sites/bernardmarr/2018/08/15/23 -fascinating-bitcoin-and-blockchain-quotes-everyone-should-read/#1e703a447e8a.

Marvin, Rob. "23 Weird, Gimmicky, Straight-Up Silly Cryptocurrencies." *PC Review,* February 6, 2018. https://www.pcmag.com/feature/358046/23-weird-gimmicky-straight-up-silly -cryptocurrencies.

Montag, Ali. "Why Cameron Winklevoss Drives an 'Old SUV' Even Though the Twins Are Bitcoin Billionaires." CNBC, January 12, 2018. https://www.cnbc.com/2018/01/12 /winklevoss-twins-are-bitcoin-billionaires-yet-one-drives-an-old-suv.html.

Nova, Annie. "Just 8% of Americans Are Invested in Cryptocurrencies, Survey Says." CNBC, March 16, 2018. https://www.cnbc.com/2018/03/16/why-just-8-percent-of-americans -are-invested-in-cryptocurrencies-.html.

Perlberg, Steven. "Bernanke: Bitcoin 'May Hold Long-Term Promise.'" *Business Insider,* November 18, 2013. https://www.businessinsider.com/ben-bernanke-on -bitcoin-2013-11.

Varshney, Neer. "Someone Paid $170,000 for the Most Expensive CryptoKitty Ever." The Next Web, September 5, 2018. https://thenextweb.com/hardfork/2018/09/05/most -expensive-cryptokitty.

Wizner, Ben. "Edward Snowden Explains Blockchain to His Lawyer—And the Rest of Us." ACLU, November 20, 2018. https://www.aclu.org/blog/privacy-technology/internet -privacy/edward-snowden-explains-blockchain-his-lawyer-and-rest-us.

Chapter 12: Wow Your Friends

All Financial Matters. "The Rule of 72, 114, and 144." May 14, 2007. http://allfinancialmatters .com/2007/05/14/the-rule-of-72—114-and-144.

Buchanan, Mark. "Wealth Happens." *Harvard Business Review,* April 2002. https://hbr .org/2002/04/wealth-happens.

Buhr, Sarah. "10 Ridiculous Kickstarter Campaigns People Actually Supported." *TechCrunch.* Accessed March 2, 2019. https://techcrunch.com/gallery/10-ridiculous-kickstarter -campaigns-people-actually-supported.

Dieker, Nicole. "Billfold Book Review: Katrine Marcal's 'Who Cooked Adam Smith's Dinner?'" *The Billfold,* June 6, 2016. https://www.thebillfold.com/2016/06/billfold-book-review -katrine-marcals-who-cooked-adam-smiths-dinner.

Godoy, Maria. "Ramen Noodles Are Now the Prison Currency of Choice." NPR, August 26, 2016. https://www.npr.org/sections/thesalt/2016/08/26/491236253/ramen-noodles -are-now-the-prison-currency-of-choice.